TH
POWER OF
MENTORSHIP

FOR THE

WOMAN
ENTREPRENEUR

Melinda Boyer

www.donboyer.org
www.DonBoyerAuthor.com

melindaboyer@realifeteaching.com

THE POWER OF MENTORSHIP
For The Woman Entrepreneur
Published by Real Life Teaching/Publishing
melindaboyer@realifeteaching.com
donboyer@realifeteaching.com
www.DonBoyer.org
www.DonBoyerAuthor.com
562-789-1909
Whittier, California

Copyright © 2007 Real Life Teaching/Publishing
Library of Congress Control Number: 2007929759
ISBN 978-1-60402-119-6

Cover Design by Mick Moore, KillerGraffix
KillerGraffix@cox.net

Editing, Composition, and Typography by Patti McKenna
Pcmckenna6@aol.com

Photos by Vics Magsaysay
vicsmag@yahoo.com

This book is available at quantity discounts for bulk purchase.
For more information contact:
Real Life Teaching/Publishing
donboyer@realifeteaching.com
Telephone: 562-789-1909
Whittier, California

Special Note: This edition of "The Power of Mentorship for the Woman Entrepreneur" is designed to provide information and motivation to our readers. It is sold with the understanding, that the publisher is not engaged to render any type of psychological, legal, or any other kind of professional advice. The content of each article is the sole expression and opinion of its author, and not that necessarily of the publisher. No warranties or guarantees are expressed or implied by the publisher's choice to include any of the content in this volume. Neither the publisher nor the individual author(s) shall be liable for any physical, psychological, emotional, financial, or commercial damages, including but not limited to special, incidental, consequential or other damages. Our view and rights are the same: You are responsible for your own choices, actions, and results.

Printed in the United States of America

Foreword

*J*erry Seinfeld once observed, "For every job, there's someone willing to do it." He then elaborated, referring to doctors specializing in unpopular parts of the anatomy. It's one of those funny lines that's only funny because it's all too true. Very few people grow up wanting to be salespeople, clerks, or sanitation workers, although we are fortunate that there are, indeed, people willing to do every job, people who try something and find they enjoy it and people who just don't know how to pursue their dreams.

Then, there is the entrepreneur. This unique individual has climbed the ladder to the high dive, hoping there will be water in the pool when they finally leap. The entrepreneur's dream begins as a thought, a mere fantasy of unattainable proportions. Then, the entrepreneur feeds the dream every day by thinking about and feeling passion for it. They season it with a dislike for their current situation and invest their emotions into it until their dream no longer seems unattainable. The entrepreneur nurtures their dream until it becomes a reality, and they wonder how they lived before, working for someone else, doing something else.

Then, there is the *woman entrepreneur!* Women, nurturing by nature, are bonded together in sisterhood with their families, girlfriends, and peers. I love speaking to groups of women. They ask interesting questions. When I share a story with them, they are right there with me--feeling what I feel. Their capacity for passion makes them tireless...working at their business in between caring for or enjoying their friends, and then back to business again.

I have been fortunate to meet many of the women who contributed to this book, like the co-founder of the Power of Mentorship series, Melinda Boyer. They all have amazing stories to share. Their strength could move mountains; and, in many cases, it has. Most women entrepreneurs have endured a hardship that men will never know; someone has told them they can't do it. Men are expected to succeed, so no one questions them when they open a business or begin a new venture. Women, on the other hand, are torn in so many directions that the respect and support of their peers and family while building a business or career are qualities that need to be earned. It's a great American tragedy.

When I decided to write my first book, "The Art of the Business Lunch," I didn't tell too many people. My friends knew I was "working on a book," but that was about the extent of it. I found that sharing my dream only served to dilute it, as well-meaning friends shared all the reasons why it would never, *could* never, become a reality.

We get pigeon-holed in the roles we play. I was thought of as an advertising account executive, the president of Women in Communication, and various other titles...I was seldom thought of as a writer. For others, like "Sally the Secretary," "Angie the Administrative Assistant," or even "Bobby's mommy and Robert's wife," breaking out of the molds others see them in can present an extra obstacle on their way to success. Some of us even need to make new friends with people who didn't know us before so we can continue to move forward with our dreams; these new friends only know us as the entrepreneurs we have become and don't question our credibility! Women have the added challenge of trying to break out of their *own* perceptions of who they are and what they should be doing with their lives. Succeeding takes a lot of faith in one's self! We must picture in our mind the person we wish to become and reprogram any negative internal dialogue.

One of the aspects of pursuing your dream that many women fail to recognize is that we have an opportunity to enrich the world with our gifts...but only if we pursue them. Our gifts are ours alone, unique and divine. Imagine if Barbra Streisand had been too shy to pursue her singing career! What if Barbara Walters accepted that broadcasting journalism was a man's world? The world would not be where it is today–filled with rich vocals and thousands of female journalists and reporters. Each of us has an obligation to pursue our passion...not just to satisfy ourselves, but because the world needs to learn our special gifts. We need to revel in our uniqueness and enjoy new experiences. How else will we be able to mentor others and share the thrills we've earned by going beyond our comfort zones?

What you hold in your hand right now is extremely powerful. This book is the blueprint for success, the encouragement to help you realize your own dreams. It is proof that those who have gone before you ventured forward in spite of their fears or reluctance and ultimately found their bliss. The women here contributed to this book and shared their stories so that they can help you. Reach out to them. We don't want you to make the same mistakes we've made. (There will be new mistakes along the way. Trust me, they help you to grow.) We want you to contribute your unique gifts and to soar.

It is my hope that you will discover your dream and the courage to pursue it, inspired by the stories in this book and by the women entrepreneurs who dared to follow their own dreams. Be uncommon....fly.

Robin Jay
www.RobinJay.com
702-460-1420
Robin@RobinJay.com

Acknowledgements

First and foremost, I want to thank my Lord and Savior Jesus Christ for He was the one who has given me life and life more abundantly. This gift allows me to use my talents and skills to their fullest potential.

I want to thank my husband, Don Boyer, for being my best friend, adviser, and life mate. Your support and encouragement inspire me to succeed.

To all our children and grandchildren who give me the drive to act on my dreams so they will feel proud of their mom and grandma for being faithful to her mission and her dreams.

To all the authors in this book who were willing to share their wisdom, experience, time, and money to help make life better for women. I'm truly honored and humbled to be associated with each and every one of you and to call you friend.

To Patricia Fripp for granting us permission to reprint "Have You Built a Business, or Just a Job?" Patricia is a speech coach, sales trainer, and speaker. Contact her at PFripp@Fripp.com.

To Marie Diamond for sharing her knowledge and expertise with our readers. You are a welcome addition to The Power of Mentorship books.

To Patti McKenna, thank you for the talents, and dedication to this book. Your editorial skills are the best in the industry!

To Mick Moore, thank you for using your talent and gifts in designing the book cover. Your friendship and contribution help us make our mission a successful one. It has been a real pleasure working with you and Manisha on this project.

To George and Olivia Ramirez for their contributions and efforts to this book, as well as the years of friendship and companionship. I look forward to many more!

To our readers and countless others who touch our lives everyday, this book would not be possible without you. Please accept our utmost gratitude and heartfelt appreciation.

Dedication

his book is dedicated to all the women throughout history who had the courage to follow their dreams and share their gifts, talents, and strengths with the world. To all the women featured in this book for choosing your higher calling and daring to make an impact through the power of your message. Thank you for being an example of a true Woman Entrepreneur.

Contents

	Introduction by Don Boyer	10
Chapter 1	The Woman Entrepreneur by Melinda Boyer	12
Chapter 2	Woman's Entrepreneurship by Jennifer Matties	18
Chapter 3	Money-What Does It Mean to You? by Kari and Lisha Schneider	24
Chapter 4	Powerful Women Have Powerful Environments by Marie Diamond	30
Chapter 5	The Forgotten Secret of Successful Women Entrepreneurs by Dr. Letitia Wright	36
Chapter 6	Are You Living in Lavish Abundance? by Glenda Feilen	40
Chapter 7	Powerful Steps for Women Entrepreneurs by DC Cordova	48
Chapter 8	How Do You Define the Woman Entrepreneur by Manisha Moore	56
Chapter 9	Slaying Dragons by Paulette Bethel	62
Chapter 10	Mentoring a Child by Lina Mack Barker	68
Chapter 11	Empowered Women, Take a Stand by Gigi Simsiman	74
Chapter 12	Making the Pieces of the Puzzle Fit by Lisa Mason DiSalvio	82
Chapter 13	Follow Your Dream by Charlotte Newbert	88
Chapter 14	Wealth Without Health? by Olivia Ramirez	94
Chapter 15	Apply the Wisdom of Your Mentors With the Right Attitude by Melissa Day	100
Chapter 16	Ten Commandments of Successful Goal Setting by Amy Nowakowski	110
Chapter 17	You are Stronger Than You Think by Anne Berryhill	118
Chapter 18	Discovering the New You by Arsenia Rendon	124
Chapter 19	To Your Health by April Dangerfield	132
Chapter 20	Have You Built a Business, or Just a Job? by Patricia Fripp	138
Chapter 21	Living Your Passion by Gail Freeman	144
Chapter 22	Follow Your Heart Song by Shauna Decker	148
Chapter 23	The Four P's for Success by Debbra Sweet	154
Chapter 24	The Worst Thing Than Can Happen to You by Robin Jay	162

Introduction

Don Boyer

*T*rue Mentorship is about training future generations to exceed and excel where we left off. It is about passing the torch of success from one generation to the next. This has been my goal, passion, and desire from day one as I created the Power of Mentorship book series. In our Power of Mentorship books, I've gathered under one roof the most powerful and influential teachers, speakers, writers, trainers, coaches, professionals, and business entrepreneurs of our day to share with you, the reader, the secrets, wisdom, and insights to make your dreams of success come true.

For the first time, it is my privilege to bring you this dynamic edition dedicated to women only. There is no doubt in anyone's mind of the powerful impact women are making in our global economy. Women today have proven with an impeccable track record and astonishing results that they play a major role in the overall success of our society, both in business and in the home.

Ask any wise and successful man, and they will readily admit that a woman (mother, spouse, or significant other) was the foundation of their accomplishments. Without my wife, Melinda, I could not have accomplished what I've done in the writing and publishing world of business. As I look back in my own personal history and at the influence women mentors play in my life today, I am most grateful.

I remember well my first girlfriend in the second grade; and from that day forward, I had the greatest respect and gratitude for God's finest creation...woman! When I was in the fourth grade, I would load up my backpack with candy bars, teddy bears, and records and would pass them out to all the sixth grade girls on the bus. Sure, all the other boys would laugh and tease me, but I didn't give a hoot. I was in the back of the bus with all the older (sixth grade) girls hugging and kissing on me!

When we had our school dance, all the boys stood against the wall with their hands in their pockets. I was on the dance floor doing the 'cha-cha" with five girls at a time! I would tell those guys, "How come you're not laughing now?" I share that with you to let you know this is one man and company that recognizes your talents, contributions, and gifts to our world.

Did you know that when a man listens, only two parts of his brain engage, but when a woman listens, seven parts of her brain are at work? What that means is, when you are talking to a man and you think he is playing dumb...most of the time, he is not playing!

From the time of creation to the 21st Century, the contribution women have made and are making to our world and society is impacting our global wealth and health, and for that...we are indebted to you.

In this edition, you will find insights and nuggets of wisdom to help you accomplish your goals and dreams. The female mentors in this book have proven that what they know and practice does work, bringing them the results they desire. The good news is what works for them, will work for you.

How do I know that? Because success is based on principles and laws, and laws and principles do not change. They are fixed and work the same way 100 percent of the time. Like gravity, they always work.

I encourage you to contact the mentors in this book and let them know how their chapter touched your life. They look forward to hearing from you. These women are real people with a heart and a desire to help you make your life a magnificent success.

Melinda Boyer

Melinda Boyer is an up and coming speaker and writer. She is the co-founder of Real Life Teaching and Real Life Publishing along with her husband, Don Boyer. She is the mother of three wonderful children, Manuel, Marco, and Marina, and is the proud grandmother of a beautiful granddaughter, "Mariah." You can contact Melinda by sending an email to her at melindaboyer@realifeteaching.com.

Chapter One

The Woman Entrepreneur

Melinda Boyer

*T*he obstacles in life can sometimes hinder you from getting where you really want to go. In 1995, I decided to go back to school and take classes that I felt I would enjoy. I am a people person and had always enjoyed working with numbers, so when I went to work for a bank, it was a natural fit for me. It seemed to me like a perfect environment; I got to work with numbers, which was fun, and had a chance to mingle with the public, which I highly enjoyed.

However, that all changed the day I was robbed. That experience began to change my perception of my job and the environment I worked in. When people walked in the bank, I now looked at them as if they were there to rob the place. Fear had taken my perception of reality and distorted it, affecting my actions and judgments. In essence, fear started holding me back from enjoying my job and life. I share this story with you to help you understand that fear not only can distort your reality, but it can hold you back from pursuing your dreams.

My Dream

My working career started at the young age of 16 years old. For the next 25 years, I found myself working for someone else. I worked for a number of great companies; nevertheless, I was building someone else's dream. There are many great advantages to working for good companies or corporate America, and for some that is a perfect fit.

But for millions of women like myself, there is an entrepreneur inside wanting to be let loose and express itself. If you are a Woman Entrepreneur or desire to be one, no matter how great the company is you work for, there is still that deep longing inside that

13

something is missing. That something is your inner desire to make your entrepreneurial mark in the world.

The global way the world does business today makes being a successful entrepreneur easier than ever before. The opportunities are endless. Unlike 25 to 30 years ago, where breaking out on your own usually required a big monetary investment and very high risk, today you can start a profitable business for $500 or less and turn that into a six-figure income in a very short time.

What does it take to be a Woman Entrepreneur? The first step is to change your mindset from a paycheck mentality to a profit mentality. Having worked the majority of my life for corporate America, my paradigm was that you had to have a JOB to survive in this world. To venture out in my own business was so scary and out of my comfort zone that I was paralyzed in my mind, even though my heart knew that was the direction I wanted to go.

When my husband and I started our company, because he had been an Entrepreneur all his life, the first area he had me work on was my mindset change. Even though our company was making more money in one month than I was making in an entire year, I still had that fear. For three months I worked harder on myself, changing my paradigms and mindset than I did on our business. But once my mindset went from a paycheck mentality to a profit mentality, I felt right at home; and I have never looked back.

Follow Your Dream

Following your dreams may require you to do some real soul searching.   There will be no doubt that as you pursue your business dreams or even your life dreams, there will be times when that journey seems too hard to follow and everything inside you cries out to stop and give up. That is when you need to dig deep within yourself and realize that you made a commitment, and no matter how many times you get knocked down, you will arise and keep moving forward.

Is following your dream always easy? No, but I've found that the reward of your dream is worth the price of every valley and hard spot you must face. When your dream is big enough and your passion strong enough, you can find a way to overcome every fear and obstacle that stands between you and that dream.

The last year on my job, right before I decided to come home to really take on the role of a Woman Entrepreneur and help build our business to a million dollar corporation, I had 10 years of the corporate world under my belt. Although I was fed up with that work environment and I was in a job where my position and department changed every quarter, there was fear when I left it. I found myself addicted to misery due to my thoughts of "What if this entrepreneurial venture doesn't work? All my benefits will be gone, and that nasty thing called a weekly paycheck will be gone, too!"

I now realize that all the misery and change that was going on in my job was really the universe giving me signs that it was time to get out of that environment and follow my dreams.

How about you? What sign is the universe giving you today? One of the best things I can share with you is that having success in life, whether it is in the arena of finances, business, home, health, or relationships, is not a byproduct of luck or good fortune, but the end result of understanding the basic laws of life. If you're going to achieve your goals and attain your dreams, you will have to implement three important factors.

1. Upgrade Your Associations

Ask yourself, "Is this the team that will get me to my dream?" If the answer is no, you must upgrade those you surround yourself with, including your mentors, associates, business partners, and friends. An important element you must understand is, "Who you listen to will determine what you have, what you get, and where you will end up," and that *is a powerful thing!*

2. Enlarge Your Thinking

You must mentally see yourself as a successful Woman Entrepreneur before you will ever experience it in your physical world. Remember, you cannot think like a poor person and expect to live like a rich person. You cannot think small and expect to live large.

Being short on money or resources does not prevent you to think like a millionaire. Thinking like a millionaire is what will change your bank account balance to a positive mode. The power of your thoughts can change every negative condition in your life to a state where your conditions reflect what you truly desire. All success begins in your thoughts; however, your thoughts are where all failure starts, as well. Enlarge your thinking to only think on things you want, and do not allow them to focus on what you do not want. Your thoughts belong to you…choose them wisely.

3. Be Visible in the Marketplace

It is not the size of your product, but the size of your market presence that determines the size of your bank account. Do you realize that there are millions of people who want what you sell? No matter what you do, someone is doing the same thing and getting rich from it. The only reason people are not knocking your door down and stuffing your bank account full of cash is they do not know how to find you. You are walking around in the marketplace of business like the invisible man. To make matters worse, you are making yourself visible to the wrong people—those who do not want your product, or do want it, but cannot afford it.

In my opinion and from our experience in business, the best way to turn a huge profit in your company or finances is to make yourself well known so that people that are pre-sold (those who want and can afford your product) can find you. Every co-author in the Power of Mentorship book series has leveraged their market presence to maximum exposure. In the last 18 months, we have put over 49,000 Power of Mentorship books into the marketplace world wide. Do you think your business might increase if your contact information, photo, and story were put in front of 49,000 people who would qualify as your target market?

This is the epitome of being visible in the marketplace so that your pre-sold customers can find you and overflow your bank account.

In closing, let me say, if you have the desire, are willing to muster up the courage and surround yourself with good mentors, you can be a successful Women Entrepreneur!

Dream, Believe, & Achieve

Jennifer Matties

Jennifer Matties, a dynamic mom of two great kids, has helped others to give birth as a Professional Birth Coach (Birth Doula), and now she helps people give birth to their dreams as a Professional Life and Success Coach and Certified Hypnotist. She is also a Trauma Intervention Specialist, providing support to people suffering the most traumatic and tragic life events. Jennifer is the Founder and Director of Life Power Group, LLC. She is also a seminar provider and dynamic public speaker and is certified to provide The Life Purpose (and Career Clarification) Process© by Fern Gorin, M.A., and the Life Purpose Institute©. Jen's real passion and power is living from the heart and teaching you to, as well. Contact her at:

Jennifer Matties
Success Coach, Hypno-Therapist
The Life Power Group LLC
www.lifepowergroup.com

Chapter Two

Woman's Entrepreneurship

Jennifer Matties CC, CHT

Creation... the act of producing or causing to exist.

*W*omen are uniquely and specially designed with the capacity for creation! We are creative and co-creators by nature's grand design! It is in our womb that new life begins, and everything about our uniqueness has been designed to support the creative process in both amazing and practical ways! We are certainly gifted and blessed in the wonderful characteristics that define our gender. When we fully realize the awesome essence of who we are and optimally unharness all our gifts, talents, and potential... we can apply our creative power in unlimited ways! We can create the life of our dreams! We can certainly apply our naturally creative tendencies and talents to the manifestation of material and entrepreneurial success in countless ways. We were born to create!

As we understand and apply the manifestation process of the Law of Attraction, we can literally take a quantum leap in our path to prosperity, abundance, and success in all areas of our lives. We don't have to understand the theories of quantum physics to make it work in our behalf! Simply stated, the Law of Attraction means that whatever we think, absolutely believe, and constantly focus on will manifest in reality. The Law of Attraction states that people experience the corresponding manifestations of their predominant thoughts, feelings, words, and actions and, therefore, have direct control over reality and their lives through thought alone. A person's thoughts (conscious and unconscious), emotions, beliefs, and actions are said to attract corresponding positive and negative experiences "through the resonance of their energetic vibration." The Law of Attraction states "you get what you think about; your thoughts determine your destiny," and, with practice, a person can use the Law of Attraction to change their life.

We live in a truly miraculous universe with amazing things happening every moment! If you feel that your desires and dreams have been elusive in any way, you need to know that unlimited resources infused with power and energy await to fulfill your every request! I firmly believe that as creators of our own reality, we have the right, the freedom, and the responsibility to consciously choose what we think, what we believe, and ultimately, the life we want to live! We are already applying these principles in our lives even when we don't know it. NOW is the time to take control and consciously and consistently use these natural laws to our greatest advantage, for ourselves and for the good of others, as well.

Entrepreneurship can be defined as: the organization, management, and assumption of risks, of a business or enterprise, usually implying an element of change or challenge and a new opportunity with reward potential. Women are naturally excellent entrepreneurs! Our innate abilities for risk tolerance, compassion, understanding, reasoning, intuition, multi-tasking, and creativity are perfect resources for managing all the unpredictable challenges and demands of any business. We want our efforts to add value and to benefit others. We seek success with balance and seek reward in holistic ways, as well as bottom-line goals. The more we as women understand what is important to us and let our feminine soul guide us, the more positive impact we can have in business and all areas of our lives.

I highly recommend that you enlist a support team to help you in your quest. Of all the strategies and tools available to help accelerate your progress, one of the most powerful and effective is mentorship! Aligning yourself with a team of mentors can inspire and propel you to success in amazing ways!

As a professional Life and Success Coach, I am absolutely convinced of the benefit of employing a coach in every step of your process and journey. A coach can help inspire you to clarify your goals with laser-like focus, help you maintain accountability, recognize and chart your progress, and encourage you to celebrate your successes along the way. It is definitely wise to engage the help of professionals in accounting, law, business, financial planning, and expert consultants in your specific field as needed.

I encourage you to use visualization, imagery, and affirmations. Acquire and implement tools to help retrain your thinking and to imagine your goals already achieved in the present moment! Here are some more helpful hints to use:

- Be clear in your desires, aware of your true motivation, and commit to your goals.
- Focus your energy and thoughts with intense and deliberate intention.
- Follow a plan and take action every day.
- Act in harmony and right action, with confidence, optimism, and purpose.
- Let go of limiting negative thoughts and fear.
- Remain flexible and adaptable.
- Have faith in the Universal Source and/or Divine Presence.
- Live with joyous enchantment, success consciousness, and an attitude of gratitude.
- Persevere with determination and NEVER GIVE UP!!!

Remember that any success or lack of it always manifests as thought in your consciousness first!

Women have the ability to multitask and are able to work, have children, raise families, and nurture great relationships. The trick to having it all is:

1. Believe it is possible.
2. Choose it to be easy.
3. Implement great time management.
4. Follow a plan and reserve the right to change your mind.
5. Work and play passionately, allowing love to flow in all you do.
6. Share your success with others and live with gratitude always.

Women instinctively want to nurture and care for others, a wonderful, selfless quality, indeed! Yet, we sometimes overlook our own needs in the process. Sometimes, we can become overwhelmed, drained, and exhausted. After juggling everything, we sometimes feel numb and unable to enjoy the process, and we find it difficult to love or accept the love coming our way.

We absolutely must take care of ourselves along the way! During the safety instructions on airplanes, we are told to put the oxygen mask on ourselves first before we attempt to assist others! If you don't take care of yourself first, how are you to take care of anyone else?

These are simple tools I use when I'm overloaded. I share these with my clients, and they have seen massive results in the way they treat their families and how they feel about themselves. My suggestion is to take some time, maybe 10 minutes or even just a few minutes everyday as time permits, at a specific time or just before walking in the door when coming home.

1. Take five deep breaths while remembering a great moment of joy, either with your child or husband, or simply something especially personally refreshing to you.

2. Feel that great feeling of appreciation you have for them being in your life, after all you chose them to be there. Or, simply be grateful for the particular joy in the memory you recalled.

3. Tell yourself three times that you're privileged to come home to your loved ones or to your own wonderful abode.

4. Walk in with your arms wide open to receive all the love your family has for you. If you are single, embrace the moment as you enter your home, hug the cat, or kiss a plant!

Take the time now to make yourself feel important. Make it a healthy habit to keep your balance and energy refreshed and rejuvenated. Now is the time to use your strengths to live and enjoy your dreams. Here are some suggestions to help you get some quality personal time.

1. Prepare your schedule for the next day the night before.

2. Do all your catching up (e-mails, client notes, facials, paint your nails) either early in the morning or at night when the kids are in bed and safe.

3. Schedule time to have lunch with a friend or partner twice a week and make sure you laugh 80% of the time.

4. Keep a gratitude journal next to your bed.

In closing, I encourage you to ask yourself a few important questions. Where do you want to go? What do you want to accomplish in your life? Are you content with your life as it currently is?

You can take control of your life and your brain, think what you want, and do what you want in this life. You can choose your own path. I encourage you to give yourself permission to live your life fully and purposely! This is it, folks. This is your experience on earth; and you can choose to stay in the same frame of mind or choose to move forward, embrace a vibrant exciting life, and truly fulfill your purpose. With the correct action steps, you will become what you want!

Be clear on where you want to go, be open to new people and opportunities coming to you. As you change and grow, so do the people you attract, as well as the opportunities presented to you. Keep your eyes and heart open for the miraculous gifts God or the Universal Divine Source Energy gives you. You receive messages everyday, whether it is through a feeling, a thought, or a physical gift. Be grateful for where you are now in life because you are in the right place right now for your unique life. Learn what you can from that place so you don't have to learn the same lesson again. Go beyond, grow, and truly become all you were born to be!

Lisha and Kari Schneider
The Twins

Lisha and Kari are so identical their own dad can't tell them apart. They've had fun doing the twin switching thing that you expect twins to do. They've also enjoyed doubling their money and fun by working together. The twins began in the entertainment field by being stunt and body doubles for Mary-Kate and Ashley Olsen. After several movies and television parts, they were introduced to the travel business, becoming top female income earners in less than a year! Lisha and Kari have been featured in national magazines as highly successful entertainers and businesswomen entrepreneurs. They also are part of a successful Entertainment Distribution Company and authors of the book *"Double Your Profits,"* a step-by-step process on how to build a fast growing business in network marketing and become financially free.

Telephone: (310) 466-8584
Email: Twins@TwinPower.biz
Website: www.TwinPower.biz

Chapter Three

$ MONEY $
What Does It Mean to You?

Lisha and Kari Schneider

*W*hat makes you happy? Whatever your answer, money is the paper and metal that happens to be the medium of exchange that will allow you to attain your long-term desires. You will need money to begin your business, to continually invest in your business, and it is what you will expect to receive for the service or product you supply. Face it, you can't be much good to yourself or anyone else unless you are prosperous. You cannot live fully without money. You were not meant to settle for lack and limitation in your life. Become the master of money. Take control of it. If you live in poverty, it controls you. You were meant to bless others and yourself with the riches of the universe.

The word MONEY provides us principles, which when put into practice, will bring you money and set your life's desires in motion.

Money
M is for Me

'**M**' is where it all begins. All personal success, without exception, begins with the M word – **Me**. You've heard it before, and it's true as can be: *If it's to be, it's up to ME!* How can a little thing like ME make such a big difference in success? Because it's ME who imagines that personal success is possible, ME who creates a plan, ME who takes the action required to sweep myself forward to success, and it's ME who must realize that the only person who really makes a difference in the quality of my life (be honest) is ME. It is not your spouse, your co-workers, your neighbors, politicians, or your friends. Don't you wish it were? Then you could blame all your failures and your under-achievements on them. Ultimately, making money starts with ME!

Which ME is it that makes the money? *Is it the ME who is born rich?* Yes–if you were born on this planet, you were born rich. We live in an abundant universe full of endless possibilities and limitless prosperity. There is plenty for everyone who wants it. We have no reason to be anything but prosperous at all times when it abounds on this planet and throughout the universe.

Is it ME who is downright lucky? Yes - you can wake up lucky every day. Luck happens when opportunity meets preparation! People make their own luck by taking advantage of every opportunity that presents itself. One person can see an opportunity and recognize it as just that, while another views the same opportunity as a problem. You become lucky when you act as if it were impossible to fail.

Is it ME who is an intellectual genius? Yes – you have all the smarts you need. More important than intellect, however, is attitude. An 'I can do it' attitude is the criterion for success. It's been said that psychosclerosis is the hardening of the attitude which causes a person to cease dreaming, seeing, thinking, and leading.

It's **any** ME who decides to do what it takes. The key word here is 'decide.' Only *you* can decide to do what it takes to achieve your dreams. Once you decide and you turn on the mental switch of total commitment, you *will* succeed, no matter what; it's just a matter of time.

It's not about deciding 'to be in business'; it's about 'deciding to succeed–no matter what!' It's about making the choice that there is only one path and to keep moving forward on that path even when you fall down or stub your toe.

MOney
The O word is Others

The '**O**' word is an absolute must. Without Others, money will never land in your bank account. All the money you are ever going to have is in *other* people's pockets. Others are the ones who decide to take it out and give it to you. Others are the ones who determine your success as much as you do.

An Equation in Success:
It's an equation that's always true.
Take one side away and it won't work for you!

$$1 \quad + \quad 1 \quad = \quad 2$$
$$Me \quad + \quad Others = \quad \$$$

Take one side away and the total outcome changes. You might ask, "What if the left side of the formula is a super-duper, powerful 'ME'? Can't I do it all by myself without the others?"

Sorry, a bigger, better '1' still makes '1'. Without 'others,' the equation would read: $1 + 0 = 1$. With this equation, you have no more than what you started with—yourself. If you have only yourself, you're not in business. There is not a lot of profit or lifestyle there! It takes ME plus OTHERS to make money.

MoNey
The N word is Now

Instead of saying TGIF, say TGIT. "Thank God it's today!"

The best way to get things done is to begin. What stops people from taking action? Why does one procrastinate? Ninety-nine percent of the time, there is only one reason. They don't *feel* like it!

One of the greatest mistakes is thinking that you should feel motivated *before* you act. There is a secret that successful people know that unsuccessful people don't. You must do something first *before* you feel like doing it. Once you begin taking action, a miracle occurs; you get a surprising little burst of emotion and suddenly realize you are enjoying the task. Motivation almost always follows action. If you don't feel like doing something, do it anyway!

Life is a DO-it-yourself program. DO is an action word. Successful people DO what unsuccessful people choose not to do.

People who take action without hesitation are those who realize that accomplishing their dreams is simply an effect of something specific that has to be done to cause it. Cause and effect is law. It is the old sowing and reaping principle. If a person is not happy with what she is reaping, it's usually because she hasn't taken charge of the sowing. You reap today what you have sown in the past. Just as a farmer has to plant specific seeds to grow specific crops, it is necessary to take specific actions to realize specific results in your life.

There is no failure in doing. There is only failure in not doing.

MonEy
The E word is Excellence

Why excellence? Because excellence demands success. You are what you repeatedly do. Excellence is not an act, but a habit. Through habits, you shape your success. A habit grows out of doing the same thing, thinking the same thing, and repeating the same words over and over again. A habit easily takes hold of your mind. After a habit has been established, it will automatically control and direct the activities of your life.

Habits can be like chains that keep you from the success you want or powerful instruments that propel you quickly toward your desires. By consciously directing your thoughts and efforts, you can change a destructive habit as soon as you discover it. Put your conscious attention on your habits and focus on replacing old destructive ones with new habits of success. Soon, you'll be unconsciously using them to bring you to your goals!

Be excellent in keeping a schedule, making a nightly 'to do list,' creating rapport with others, investing in what is important to you, being kind to yourself, making healthy choices, and being flexible.

MoneY
The Y words are Yes, I can!

Yes, I can is the winning attitude that will take you wherever you want to go. There is no wrong side of the bed. You get up on the wrong side of your mind. Choose to get up on the right side of the bed everyday.

Yes, I can is the attitude that will unlock doors which will take you where you desire. It's the attitude that result-oriented people understand.

Yes, I can is the attitude of a woman who doesn't find fault, but one who finds a remedy.

Yes, I can is the attitude of a woman who never gives up. It is acquired by the changes that occur inside. It's been said that the highest reward for a person's toil is not what he gets for it, but what he becomes by it.

Yes, I can is the attitude of a woman who continually thinks of herself as rich and successful. She is consciously aware of prosperous thinking and implants the feeling of richness in her mental atmosphere.

Develop a *Yes, I can* train of thought on which to ride. It will take you in a direction that will give you power to change your life. The doors to your great success will open wide, and this attitude will allow you to walk through them with confidence and joy.

Life is not a dress rehearsal.
Make the most of it by using MONEY

M – Me
O – Others
N – Now
E – Excellence
Y – Yes, I can!

Marie Diamond

Marie Diamond, teacher featured in The Secret, an internationally known Feng Shui Master, and one of the top transformational leaders in the world, consults with and teaches people in more than 147 countries. Marie has connected with numerous Hollywood celebrities, major film directors and producers, music giants, and famous authors. Her current projects include writing books, consulting, speaking engagements, TV shows and educational movies, creating several large real estate projects, and the creation of an e-commerce site. Contact Marie at:

www.MarieDiamond.com
Email: Info@MarieDiamond.com

Read her blog at:
http://mariediamondblog.blogspot.com

Chapter Four

Powerful Women Have Powerful Environments

Marie Diamond

*T*hrough my work, I've had the chance to meet powerful women. Among them are female billionaires, female politicians who made a difference in their countries, female self-improvement teachers, female rock and roll icons, top models, and powerful women who are not noticed by the media.

Powerful Women

When a woman lives her full passion with the freedom to express herself, then I consider her to be powerful. These women made it happen for themselves. Interestingly enough, they always included their family and their community in their growth.

I encountered them when they asked me as a Feng Shui Master and spiritual advisor to support them in their personal life and business projects. Most of these women didn't have one mentor—they had a whole group of advisors around them, from all different levels of interests.

In my interview with them, I always ask, "Who are your advisors, your helping hands, your mentors?" Then, I try to express these people in their environment.

The women I saw had mentors helping them on a physical level: their personal doctor or healer or trainer. They also had emotional mentors: their mom or sisters, girlfriends in their local network, a psychologist, or even sometimes their hairdresser.

The mental mentoring happened most of the time through coaches, books, audio CDs and, if they had time, attending a workshop. But,

31

books were where they got most of their answers and information, from mentoring them to inspiring them with new ideas. And they always had a spiritual mentor: a priest, a guru, a spiritual advisor, or praying or meditation.

I found that they had an all-around mentorship program, much different than men. Most men didn't have the emotional mentorship in place. They didn't share their emotions and feelings and ask for advice on that level from someone. That is perhaps the reason why powerful women have fewer heart attacks; they share more of what is in their hearts than powerful men.

Another interesting part that I encountered is that they wanted their team to know each other. They were not afraid to share who the other players in their supporting team were. We know each other's names, and when possible, we meet each other.

Powerful women are like queens. They need court ladies surrounding them. I've met many women who acted like queens. But powerful women always act like queens with a heart, compassionate to themselves and toward the ones supporting them.

They share with the court ladies their abundance, their gifts, their sorrow, and laughter. It is like a group of girlfriends all directed to the benefit of the queen, as she has the greatest impact on the world. Her advisors, who act as the court ladies, are happy to support the queen because through her work, they reach the world, too.

Powerful Women Have Powerful Environments

The home for women is more personal than for a man. Powerful women organize their work environment like their home. They need to feel at home where they work. When you look in offices of men and women, more personal images or connections will hang or stand out in the office of women.

I have seen women really follow their intuition where they wish to work the most. When a man is given a desk, he will work there, even if energetically the place is not that great. But, women will feel if the desk is supporting her or not.

When I give advice to my female clients, I always use my diamond dowsing techniques. Dowsing is a technique to find the strongest energetic spot in a home or office. By the impact of geopathic stress (undercurrent water or fault lines) or electromagnetic fields, a place can be contaminated and create concentration and inspiration problems. Ninety percent of modern buildings have problems with this. It is easily curable, and everyone can learn how. What I encounter is that powerful women have such a great sense for their environment that they will intuitively look for the best place in their office or home to work from. When I check their places out, the place that has the least stress is the place where they sit working on their laptop, making their phone calls, negotiating, working out their plans, etc.

I know a powerful self-improvement teacher, and she always works from her kitchen island. It is the place in her whole home with the least amount of stress. She had the good luck to also have a positive vortex (a point where the ancient masters built the temples, the cathedrals, and the castles), and she admitted that many great inspirations and projects were born right there on the kitchen island. Unfortunately, not everyone has a positive vortex in their office or home; but you can create one.

The point is women are drawn to such a place to do their work. My experience shows that their environment is playing a larger role in their power than they imagine.

Power Position

In order to be in a position of power in your company or in your profession, you need to start at your office or at home by placing yourself in a power position. A power position means that from where you sit you can see the incoming flow, the people walking in.

Power Chair

Choose a powerful chair: a high-backed chair with arm rests—just like a throne. You can't express power without having the right chair to sit on. You are the empress of your empire. Even if your empire is a small business or your household, you still need to be the one with strength. Power is not about control; power is about strength. Also, women entrepreneurs have so many levels of attention that they can use all the focus.

Be Supported in Your Power

Women, more than men, need extra support. Make sure you have a wall behind you where you work, or even a plant. If you are sitting in a vulnerable position, you definitely need a strong, powerful chair. On the wall behind you, you can also hang an image of a mountain or of people who support you, like your mentors or a spiritual image like angels, a Buddha, or any image that reflects divine support.

Diamond Space Feng Shui

Your environment is the reflection of who you are. There is a wind direction that supports you personally to be successful as women; it is the place where you put your vision board, hang your logo, and place your products. In order to learn this, email us at info@mariediamond.com, provide your birthday (year, month and day) and we will tell you your success direction.

Generally, in the southwest area of your office, you can also place images of successful women entrepreneurs: women who have walked the path before you and made a success of their life or of their vision.

Collaboration

One of the aspects of business that women need to focus on is collaboration. I always suggest women connect with a mastermind group so they don't feel alone as women in business. You can stimulate collaboration by placing an item of a fuchsia color in the southwest area of your office. Hang a team picture up or business cards of people who support you in your personal relationship direction.

Stimulate collaboration to create a more powerful environment. A powerful environment creates a more powerful you!

Dr. Letitia S. Wright, D.C

Dr. Letitia S. Wright, D.C. is the host of the Wright Place™ TV Show, the fastest growing business lifestyle show on broadcast television today. Dr. Wright introduces women to the experts, products, strategies and events that will help them grow their business. She features experts like Mark Victor Hansen, Stedman Graham, Robert G. Allen, and Marie Diamond, as well as stars like Terry Hatcher and Marla Gibson.   Dr. Wright can be reached at:

www.wrightplacetv.com

Pick up your special gift at:
www.pomwe.com

Chapter Five

The Forgotten Secret of Successful Women Entrepreneurs

Dr. Letitia S. Wright, D.C.

*E*ach year, thousands of new businesses fail. This year alone, over 100,000 women will fail at their current business. They will not make a million dollars, they will not get any awards, they will not be recognized on the street, and they won't be a guest on Oprah. As they try and analyze what happened, most women will miss the real cause of business failure. No one will tell them about the secret business killer.

There are a few key things you must know and implement in order to have a successful business. These are not taught by SBA or business schools, even though they are imperative to your success as a female entrepreneur. When these things are not addressed, failure is the only outcome to expect. When these things are not taken care of, you work extremely hard for very little gain. When you have no mechanism to handle these items, your business will leave you tired, overworked, and joyless. Your business becomes a constant source of exhaustion and embarrassment.

FAILURE FOCUS: A BUSINESS KILLER

It's not your mistakes that kill your business; it's your focus on your mistakes that can kill your business. If you have failed, put it behind you. Make a list of ten things you learned from them. Focus on that and not on the fact that you failed. Focus on what you learned, and the failure will work for you. You now have something to celebrate because you will never do those things again. Successful people spend very little time remembering and reminding themselves of their failures. Many literally forget about it. Because the focus is on what they learned, they spend no time blaming themselves. They do not use their time feeling sorry for themselves.

If failure haunts you, you must find a way to move on. This is what truly successful people do.

THE SUPER-SECRET HIDDEN CAUSE
OF BUSINESS SUCCESS

Many women start their own businesses while still working another job or while raising their families. Even with only a part-time job, when you add a business into your life, your cup is spilling over. Just imagine, you have an entire household you are responsible for, and then you add a business on top of it. Even if you are a single woman, you have a full life to which you are adding a new business. You do not feel the overload at first because you're naturally excited about your business. But then overload causes other areas of life to start failing.

Women must add support to their lives. Women need real practical support. I am not talking about delegating more work to your spouse and children. This results in creating overload in their lives. Besides, who says this is how they want to spend their time? I am talking about support for you. This may mean bringing in a housekeeper or a virtual assistant. It could mean having real meals planned and precooked by someone else. It could mean getting help with laundry. There are only so many hours in a day. You need assistance. Men have no problem adding this kind of support to their lives. They will hire someone to take care of the lawn and pool because they don't have time. They bring in someone to fix things because they don't have the time. They want to spend their time doing things they enjoy, not more chores. So, they delegate the chores and add more hours to their lives. Women must learn to do the same.

When I hear a woman tell me that she is a single parent starting her own business and has no one to help her, my heart aches. These women are trying to make calls with their pets and children screaming and running in the background. This makes them sound unprofessional on the phone. Their business work is on the kitchen table; they don't even have a private desk for their work. This means the family cannot sit down for a meal together, or she has to constantly move what she's working on and interrupt her progress.

Lack of support is the biggest hidden cause for failure for the woman entrepreneur because you cannot run a successful business while the rest of your life falls apart. This secret works for everyone, whether you are a work-at-home mom or not.

I know of two stay-at-home moms who met at the local park. They saw each other occasionally, and over time, they struck up a conversation. They got to know and like each other. It turns out they only lived a block away from one another. One mom was a home-schooling mom. The other was a stay-at-home mom who was trying to create and grow an online business. They both felt a little overwhelmed and decided to give each other the gift of support. They did not have extra money or a lot of extra time, so they decided to start small. In order to make it manageable, the moms decided to exchange two hours a week. Each week, they babysat each other's children for two hours.

The home-school mom had time to take a long hot bath, eat a late lunch with her friends, read, or do whatever she needed to refresh herself. Her goal was to have a little time to herself. The mom with the online business wanted two hours to work on her business. She didn't want to stay up all night working on it. She wanted uninterrupted time, while her mind was fresh, to create her website. These two hours every week gave her time to develop her business. She started making money and then began reinvesting some of her profits into other kinds of support so she could have more time to grow her business without sacrificing her family time.

You can be creative. Talk to others around you; find out what their needs are. Perhaps you can meet them with a simple trade. This simple trade can support you as you grow your business. This gift can support you in simply living the life you really want.

As you grow your business, give yourself the gift of success. Forget about your failures. Give yourself the gift of real support.

Glenda Feilen

Glenda Feilen, author, speaker, and recognized authority on the law of attraction, shares no-fail techniques to achieve prosperity and success in her book, "*Are All Your Pieces In Place*." For over 25 years her books, seminars, and workshops have taught thousands an empowering process to achieve wealth, happiness, and rewarding relationships based on the law of attraction. Her mission is to show others how to employ simple, easy techniques to attract tremendous abundance and success in every aspect of their lives. Also a personal design consultant, Glenda's "Fashion for the Soul" workshops teach women to look and feel fabulous when they dress so their natural radiance shines through. They instantly see changes in their lives when they recognize colors, patterns, styles, and designs that communicate to the world who they really are. She is a nutritional expert and has been a marketing director for over 25 years in an international nutritional based corporation. Glenda is available for speaking engagements. Her 'Law of Attraction' and 'Fashion for Soul' workshops are life changing and fun, fun, fun! Learn more about the laws of abundance by purchasing her CD set, *You Want it? You Got it!* on her website at www.ContactGlenda.com.

Email: Glenda.f@cox.net
Telephone: (619) 749-2075

Chapter Six

Are You Living in Lavish Abundance?
Learn to Deliberately Create Wealth

Glenda Feilen

*Y*ou mean there are universal laws about creating wealth? You bet! Live them and claim the wealth that is waiting for you!

How would you feel if a never-ending supply of money poured into your life?

Are you striving for a life of prosperity? Do you have any area of lack in your life right now? Do you have a shortage of anything? Are you in debt? Do you wish you had a savings and money to give away?

If you said "Yes" to any of those questions, I have good news for you! There is a simple easy solution to attract wealth and abundance and create the life of your dreams.

Do you Thrive - or just Survive?

Why aren't *you* wealthy? Why isn't *everyone* wealthy? *Why do most people barely survive, rather than thrive?* We live in a world of abundance. Abundance is a natural state in our universe. Do you think maybe it's because you aren't lucky? Fewer than 20% of today's millionaires inherited even a small portion of their wealth. Of those who inherited, or even won the lottery, more than 80% were bankrupt within 5 years. So, it's obviously not luck.

Could it be that maybe you are not intelligent enough? Most of today's millionaires didn't graduate with high honors, and many didn't even go to college because they couldn't qualify. I guess intelligence isn't the answer.

If it's not luck and not being super smart that makes us wealthy, what is it that the wealthy know that the people who aren't wealthy don't know? They understand the laws, the principles of accumulating wealth and keeping it.

There are laws. They are Universal Laws; and just as the law of gravity affects each of us, whether we understand it or not, these Universal Laws of Prosperity affect our daily finances and level of prosperity in every aspect of our lives. No matter who you are, if you live the law—you reap the benefits; if you don't—you won't.

LAWS OF PROSPERITY:

1. **There is no Receiving without ASKING**
   Asking begins the creating process. When you ask, you are mentally entertaining something. If you can't conceive something or choose something, then you have no desire. Put your desires into formality by deliberately and consciously asking. Only when you develop the state of mind where you can ask for something, can you develop the state of mind where you can achieve it. Asking occurs in many ways:

   • You ask the universe for what you want when you handwrite your specific, positively-stated goals. Make sure you write them so they give you an emotional charge every time you write them.

   • You ask the universe by supplying your mind with specific pictures in which you see yourself having already attained your desire. Run mental previews of what you want to manifest in your physical life.

   • You ask the universe by creating a private goal chart with specific, goal-related pictures placed on it, personalized with your own picture.

- You ask the universe by stating to yourself and others positive words that affirm the things you want are presently occurring.

- You ask by handwriting affirmations nightly, which deeply impress your mind just before you sleep.

2. The LAW OF ATTRACTION

Everything in the universe works with the law of attraction. There is a current of energy that runs through everything on this planet and in this universe. It is the basis of our world, and it is the basis of you.

Everything is energy. We live in a vibrational universe. You are an energy being as much as you are a physical being. Recognizing that everything vibrates at a particular frequency or rate of speed is a vital part of understanding how to attract prosperity to you. Waves of living energy literally radiate from your body. They ripple and flow and merge with other waves. They are like a radio signal, emitting your words, thoughts, and feelings; and those things which are on the same vibrational frequency of that which you emit are returned to you.

You are held accountable energetically by this law of attraction. Life is a mirror giving you feedback on the vibrations you are sending through your thinking, feelings, and actions. This means your daily experiences, the situations you experience, the people in your life, everything around you, matches your vibrational radiations outward.

Even though you think money is nothing more than metal and paper with numbers on it, money is a system of energy. Everything is a system of energy and works with the law of attraction! Money is neutral, and the energy you give it is the energy it takes on in your life.

Am I saying that you can be a deliberate creator of what you want in your life by controlling the vibrations that emanate from you? Absolutely! That's the point. You are the sole creator of your life, and it is time to create the things you want. Consciously create the amount of money you want. You are putting yourself in a vibrational place of either receiving exactly what you want or what you don't want by what you radiate outward.

Thoughts are things which radiate to the world how you feel about money. Nothing can occur in your life without the initiation of it through a thought. Never think of yourself as poor or needy. What you think about comes about. What you focus on is what you get. Don't think about how little you have or how much less you'll bring in to pay the bills that you have. Think about how much you have and how you will feel when you have a surplus. You get more of what you focus on, so focus on what you want, not what you don't want. Never think that you have to work hard to make money or that money isn't happiness, or that having money is being 'filthy' rich. Never think that being poor is synonymous with being humble. Money is not the root of all evil; George Bernard Shaw said, "Lack of money is the root of all evil." Think positively about money! Rather than thinking of how little you have, think about how much you have. Think thoughts that bring you prosperity, and deliberately choose those thoughts.

Words create! Never say, "I can't afford it," "Money doesn't grow on trees," "It costs too much," or "I'll never get ahead." These are words of lack. When you say these things, you'll be right!

The minute you begin changing these words, your poverty consciousness is being changed. Use words of success. Change your words to "I now choose lavish abundance for myself," "I always have enough," "I'm comfortable with large amounts of money," "Money is my friend," "Money effortlessly flows to me," "I see money effortlessly flowing to me," "I see prosperity everywhere," and "I give thanks for (what you want more of)."

As you say these things, your mind (which naturally thinks in pictures) creates pictures to go with your words. If your finances are currently out of control, your thoughts and words are also out of control. You must change your habitual thoughts and words immediately.

3. **You must CREATE A VACUUM**
    If you want to receive something, you must make room for it. Nature abhors a vacuum. Whenever something is released and a vacuum is created, the universe makes sure that something is immediately sucked into that area. Remove every thought and word of lack, poverty consciousness, of money not being good, and of not being deserving. Even though these are habitual, you can consciously replace them with words and thoughts of prosperity. The more you change your habits, the less frequently thoughts and words of lack will occur.

    Clean out your closets and drawers; clean up your car. Everything around you, especially your home environment, mirrors your inner self. Clutter accumulates when energy stagnates; and, likewise, energy stagnates when clutter accumulates. When you give away and release things you no longer need, it opens your life for things you desire to come in.

    Eliminate any toxic emotions you are holding onto. Anger, resentment, guilt, envy, regret, criticism, and other similar emotions block your prosperity. Release others and yourself from these emotions. Replace them with forgiveness, acceptance, willingness, understanding, love, joy, serenity, peace, and enlightenment. You do not forgive for others. You forgive for you.

    You can only attract to yourself what you are. The highest thing that you will attract to yourself is influenced by the lowest feeling you have about any person, place, or thing. Set yourself free, and you will immediately attract people and situations into your life that will prosper you.

4. You Must GIVE to Receive!

Sometimes people want to receive *before* they give. It doesn't work that way. Let's do a little experiment: Fold your arms. There you are all closed up, hugging yourself. Are you in a position to receive? I think NOT. Now extend your arms forward as if you were in a position to give. Look, you are in exactly the right position to receive. Again, there is an energy flow. What goes out comes back; and *no matter how little you have, you always have something to give.*

Give others thoughts of prosperity. See them accomplishing their goals. When you give them thoughts of abundance and prosperity, you are actually giving to yourself those similar vibrations of abundance and prosperity and the things you want. Shoot others with thoughts of prosperity secretly, and you will see that you are secretly putting those things into play in your life.

Give gratitude and appreciation. Give thankfulness for what you have and what you expect to have in the future. Constantly look for things and others to praise. Be generous with what you have. Give love and support to others. Treat yourself lavishly. Use your best on yourself. Bask yourself in abundance. Get rid of habits of scarcity. Spend money. Money must flow. What you put out comes back to you multiplied, and this applies to money as well as everything else in your life.

5. Take INSPIRED ACTION

You must TAKE ACTION if you want prosperity! You often hear the saying "Attitude is everything." Wrong. The "A" word that makes all the difference is "Action." You can have a great attitude about everything, but if you sit on the beach all day and take no action, you will not achieve prosperity.

The power to create is given by Divine Intelligence. You are One Energy with the Master Creator; and when you use this type of creative energy, you know it because your actions are inspired. Your life flows with synchronicity. Everything falls together perfectly. Creative energy is joyful energy, and you are an extension of that energy. Therefore, it is vital to take action that is fun, exciting, interesting, and inspiring. Do the things that give you joy. Laugh when you work. Listen to fun or inspiring music. Create a beautiful environment. It is the light fun energy that creates. Menial, boring tasks will not bring what you want into your life.

When you do the things you love, money will pour into your life. Your actions will not feel like work. They will be play. While you are taking action, feel the feelings you would feel if you already had all the money you wanted.

Implementation of knowledge is power. Now that you know the laws, make tiny, little behavior changes, and you will begin to see the results appear in your life. If you do the same thing— you're going to have the same thing. If you want something different, you have to do something different.

It is simple to put these laws into action. All change begins with choice. Make a decision; choose right now to be wealthy. Make a decision to take advantage of the abundance that is already yours and is just waiting for you to claim it! There are no excuses. Being in poverty is equivalent to being a victim. Being a victim is allowing something or somebody to direct your life. If you want the lack of money to direct your life, you're a victim and will find an excuse not to live the Laws of Abundance.

If you live these Universal Laws of Abundance, the universe has no choice but to respond by supplying you lavish abundance. If you obey the laws, you get the benefits. Nobody wakes up in the morning and says, "Today, I choose to be broke" or "Today, I choose to fail." But, you are choosing that by not choosing to create the opposite, which is to live the Universal Laws of Abundance. Live them to the fullest, and you *will* have a never-ending supply of money pouring into your life.

DC Cordova

DC Cordova, a pioneer of high-speed, experiential, entrepreneurial education, co-founded organizations that present the famous *Money & You® Program* and *Excellerated Business Schools® for Entrepreneurs,* an international organization with over 65,000 graduates from the Asia Pacific and North American regions. She is a "Connector" because she has a special gift for bringing the world together. *Excellerated Entrepreneurial Portal™* is being developed as an "Entrepreneurial Connector". DC is a partner with Willson Lin of Doers Group and part of a television program based on the *Excellerated Business School®* which has been shown through CETV. Among her graduates are wealth/business gurus, including her past business partner, Robert Kiyosaki of the *Rich Dad/Poor Dad* Series. DC is a *Mentor of Nurturing* and *Ambassador of New Education* because of her tireless pursuit to transform educational systems around the world and eradicate poverty and hunger. Contact DC at http://www.excellerated.com or at http://www.dccordova.com Phone: 1-619-224-8880.

Chapter Seven

Powerful Steps for Women Entrepreneurs

DC Cordova

As little as 40 years ago, there were few female entrepreneurs in the world–they were the exception, rather than the rule. It was assumed that women with money had either married into it or inherited it—very rarely that they had actually earned or made it themselves. Because of the more open attitudes of the last few decades, women's real contribution to business, politics, economics and world affairs in general are being more exposed and celebrated.

Today, women are in search of a balance between job and family. They also want freedom from sex-based barriers in corporate life and economic survival. So, women are going into business for themselves at higher rates than men are. The fact is that women are still not as readily accepted in the male-dominated world of business. This is sometimes an advantage because it helps propel them to the top more quickly.

Small business, in particular, has become the economic proving ground for women. In the 70's, women owned fewer than 5% of businesses. Women are no longer willing to be limited by the well-documented "glass ceiling." Women now own more than one-third of small businesses in the United States, with the numbers rising yearly. Women-owned firms operate in all sectors of the economy – wholesale, retail, finance, insurance, real estate, education, manufacturing, transportation and others—and over half are in services. While it is a new occurrence, women have made their own fortunes and built big businesses.

The great thing about the *Information Age* and technology is that when doing business over the Internet, the gender of the person is not an issue. A woman can literally set up her business from a dining room table, transact business internationally, and be very successful without incurring any prejudice or preconceived notions about her capabilities. This benefit is now enjoyed by many female entrepreneurs regardless of race, age, or any physical disabilities that may have limited them in the past. The *Information Age* truly is changing many things for the better.

Mentors and Role Models

If you look at the movies made in the 50's and early TV, the Doris Days, Marilyn Monroes, Debbie Reynolds, and Rosalind Russells were the role models of women. They got what they wanted by being cute, sexy, subservient, and – unfortunately, at times – very dumb. Then in the '70's and '80's, the pendulum swung. The feminist role models admired were masculine, aggressive, macho-like and angry "for the way women had been treated."

Now, even in developing nations, savvy women know that the key to surviving in the business world is to create networks and support groups of like-minded people who will help them succeed. Men have been creating "good old boys networks" for years. Women are now taking the best of those models and making it work for them. The number of "women networks" are going through the roof. All business people who are going places know that one of the best ways to get started in business is to network with other successful business people—and in certain fields, particularly with women.

In our network of successful entrepreneurs around the world, the *Excellerated Business Schools®* and *Money and You®* Programs have some amazing female entrepreneurs. An example of one is our friend and mentor, Dr. Dato' Jannie Tay, owner of The Hour Glass – a fine watch chain with outlets in Malaysia, Singapore and Australia. She has been named one of the top 25 Female Asian Entrepreneurs, one of the 50 Most Successful Business Women in the world, and is one of the top Chinese Entrepreneurs as rated by several different global organizations and magazines.

Another friend, Datuk Maznah Hamid, the "Iron Lady" of Malaysia, is the co-founder and owner of one of the most successful security businesses in Asia, Securiforce, with her own "army" of nearly 4,000 security officers at her disposal. She also serves in the Ministry of Entrepreneurship for the Malaysian Government, advising women and men how to start and succeed in their own businesses. In addition to running her company, she carries out an active career speaking to and motivating women all over Malaysia and throughout Asia. These amazing entrepreneurs help other women. They contribute to their local and global communities. They are constantly working to help and empower people to go into business for themselves. They demonstrate to other women that not only can they succeed fully in having a happy family life, but they can become prosperous in business, too.

Find Role Models

Do you know women who demonstrate a balanced life with good relationships, happy families, and a successful career or business? If so, those are the women from whom you want to learn.

Find men who truly wish to empower women to be all that they can be. Women must learn to surround themselves with empowering men. They must know who they should listen to and who can be counted on for support.

The most powerful people on earth—referring to personal power and not necessarily political or financial power—are people who know their strengths and weaknesses. Women must accept that a stereotypical perception may precede them. You may be subjected to people who will wonder (or ask) if it is your "time of the month." People will ask if you are married, if you're a single parent, or even if you "slept your way" into your job. These are questions that are never asked of a man. The more women understand this mentality and have a polite way to deal with it, the better off they will be.

Women do have to work harder to get to the top. Don't let the message upset you. Be willing to take off your rose-colored glasses and set aside your wishful thinking of how the world "ought to be." Look around you and ask other women about how the business environment really is in your field, area, and country. Don't let the small minority of famous and well-known women who have become successful (and very wealthy) fool you into thinking everyone gets to the top easily. You only know about them because you see them in the media. These women worked very hard to get to where they are today... and so can you!

It is Important to Study Your Field

Find out the percentage of women in your field with positions of importance. Find a mentor who will advise you on the best steps to take in your field in order to succeed. Set yourself up financially and legally so that, from the start, there is equal ownership according to the law, with your partner(s)–even if it's your husband. There are far too many cases around the world where women made major sacrifices, made their partner rich and/or famous, yet have nothing to show for it. Many women are expected to take a smaller share just because they are married or in a non-partner relationship with a man. After 10 years, there is nothing on paper to show it, and it looks like she did not contribute at all!

Luckily, in the 21st century, we are now putting women to work, side by side with young men who have been brought up by women born in the 60's and later. This group of males has less of a judgmental attitude and most don't see themselves as superior to women as some of their fathers did. Unfortunately, many of these men are not in power—yet—but later in the 21st century they will be, and our daughters will have a much better chance to fully express themselves in the world of business.

What Steps Should a Woman Take?

Here are steps that a woman can take to not only become an awesome entrepreneur but also a powerful human being:

Educate yourself in relevant education. The most important and best tool for women is entrepreneurial, "real life" education. Learn the basics of what a good entrepreneur needs to know in order to be successful in business: *Sales/Marketing; People/Organization; Money/Finances.* One of the greatest secrets is to empower yourself with knowledge and apply it with maturity and wisdom. Take classes, participate in seminars, read business/marketing/personal growth books, listen to educational materials, and research topics of interest in the Internet. Read world affairs magazines such as *Time* and *Newsweek.* Read business magazines such as *BusinessWeek, Fortune* and *Fast Company* with the latest financial and Internet news. This is not a choice if you want to succeed in life. You must be able to hold a conversation in any circle.

Use tools that support you. There are wonderful tools out there that can help you identify your strengths and weakness, what you are best at, and how to work effectively with others. The *DISC Profile* is one of those great tools that has supported many in finding what they are best at. There is the *Passion Test* to find your heart's desires. Find the tools that will empower and support you.

Surround yourself with people who support you. Choose mentors and people who will guide you, tell you the truth and ask more of you than you ask of yourself. It's not a good habit to surround yourself with people who limit your goals or want you to live up only to their expectations. Once you begin to grow, you may become challenging to those that don't want to.

Build your financial independence. Separate at least part of your finances from your husband or partner. Build your assets and your financial portfolio in a way that it can clearly be divided should anything go wrong. Talk about and plan for it openly. Educate yourself about money, business, and finances. Have clear rules of the game and policies on what happens (1) if your business partner or spouse passes away, (2) if you want to leave the relationship, or (3) if your partner leaves the relationship.

Learn how to work with your emotions effectively. While women's emotions are also their strength, being highly emotional in certain environments can be considered a weakness. The more you clear past emotional blocks, the more powerful you will be. Find a program and work with mentors/coaches who will teach you how to work with your emotions in a way that support you in stressful situations.

Do everything you can to empower other women. Do not compete with other women under any circumstances. Do whatever you can to support each other and reach your dreams and goals.

Teach your children, especially your sons, to love, support and empower women to ensure men support future generations of women. Most cultures still teach boys to have a "macho" standard that encourages men to be more competitive and to think of winning, no matter at what cost. Counter this by teaching them win/win attitudes. Teach and encourage them to get in touch with their feelings and express them responsibly.

Don't act dumb or play "victim." With all due respect to a wonderful actress, the "Marilyn Monroe" days are over. Unfortunately, her characterizations of women in movies did a lot of damage to women—and she, incidentally, was humiliated beyond imagination. Whenever you think you have it tough, read books such as Suzanne Sommers' biography about her struggle with her "bimbo" image in Hollywood a few decades ago. Just imagine what it must have been like being blacklisted in Hollywood for refusing to play a bimbo in those days. Suzanne stuck to her guns and years later had one of the most successful direct selling stories in history. She became independently wealthy not only by playing it smart, but also by letting go of blocks that were in her way of being successful. Bookstores – the Internet – are full of great inspirational stories like hers. Google it!

Let go of guilt. If you work full-time running a business, let go of the guilt of having to hire people to work for you. Remember that you are contributing to someone else's ability to earn a living. It was another era that women were meant to stay home and raise children. The economics of today's world don't allow many to stay at home. Get the help you need to succeed in whatever endeavor you embark on. Having household help is a necessity. A man wouldn't think of working at home without appropriate support to keep the house and family running smoothly – so why should you?

Find a business you can do from home. In increasing numbers, women who do not have traditional jobs are going into businesses they can operate from home. There are huge opportunities for women in home-based businesses. Do your market research—you'll find what is perfect for you.

And teach your daughters all of the above.

In 1997, we were saddened by the death of two leading, internationally known women, Princess Diana and Mother Teresa. We are reminded that women can open people's hearts as no one else can. Women are uniting the masses—yes, sometimes in sorrow—but we are all discovering that our feminine qualities such as compassion, holding a loving attitude toward all, and lending a hand can make a world of difference to others. While the world mourned the loss of these two extraordinary women, Princess Diana and Mother Teresa's qualities were what the entire world remembered. This made people stop and reflect on the tremendous influence that powerful and loving women have. Perhaps it was no accident that, within weeks of their passing, global entrepreneur Ted Turner donated 1 billion U.S. dollars to the United Nations!

Be committed as a woman to be all that you can be, for as Goethe said: *"Whatever you can do, or dream you can . . . begin it. Boldness has genius, power and magic in it."* You are welcome to download the rest of this wonderful poem from our website: www.excellerated.com/commitment.

I wish you tremendous success – and remember, every morning is a new opportunity to start all over; and if you are not the happiest that you can be—choose that—and the world will become a different place and new doors will open for you!

Manisha Moore

Manisha (Moua) Moore is an Entrepreneur, Chef, and Internet Expert. Manisha is also the Vice President of Sales and Marketing and Network Administrator for KillerGraffix, a prominent design and marketing group based in San Diego, California. To learn more or to contact Manisha, visit:

www.mishacuisine.com
www.passionfruitbaby.com
www.killergraffix.com

Chapter Eight

How Do You Define the Woman Entrepreneur?

Manisha Moore

H ow do you define the woman entrepreneur? I believe the answer to this question transcends beyond the business world we all associate with today.

Being an entrepreneur comes in many forms and is driven by different needs. It's not just about making money, but for a woman, it's an innate need to provide, nurture, and give.

I am a Hmong woman, born in Laos and raised in the United States. In my culture, women are enterprising by default out of a necessity for survival. Women lived in segregated societies where men and women do not eat together and are not treated as equal. However, it was the woman's role to nurture and provide for the family.

This cultural tradition instilled an entrepreneurial spirit in my upbringing at a very young age. My grandmother said I was sautéing over an open flame at the tender age of three. This sounds unbelievable, but it explains how I could cook for a family of 8 at the age of 12. The women of my culture are taught to be self sufficient at a very young age, so being an entrepreneur came to me naturally.

One can only imagine what life was like for women at the beginning of the 20th century. They couldn't vote. Women in my culture had to walk behind men and still do to this day in the old country. They were likely to die in childbirth and educational opportunities were limited. Women were barred from most professions and were treated like second class citizens.

We have certainly come a long way. I have multiple successful businesses of my own, and my fellow Hmong sister, Mee Moua, is a U.S. Senator from Minnesota.

There has never been a better time than the present to be an entrepreneur, especially a woman entrepreneur. With unbelievable advances in technologies available today, along with the evolution of the Internet, being a woman entrepreneur has never been easier or as abundant with opportunities.

There are specialized women network groups of every conceivable interest. All you have to do is search online, find something you are interested in and signup. Joining a network group or starting your own network is one of the many ways you can jump start your business or get your feet wet. You'll quickly see that there are thousands of like-minded women entrepreneurs out there seeking knowledge and business alliances just like you.

With the Internet, it's easy to market any business idea or just share your ideas freely with a global reach.

Today's women entrepreneurs are using the Internet, networking and technology such as podcasting to broadcast their products and services to the world with little or no startup cost. We all know that advertising on radio and TV can be extremely cost prohibitive. However, you can build an entire store online with virtual inventory, broadcast your own show and have the best time slots of your choosing. Ten years ago, this would not have been possible.

Today, we have many amazing high-tech communication devices equipped with mobile technologies that allow us to communicate and do business anytime, anywhere. With the ability to advertise directly to cell phone users, podcasting is just a small example of this emerging technology.

I would like to share a podcasting success story about the endless opportunities available to you on the Internet.

Mommycast.com was a show started by two moms. Their purpose was to share tips with other women on the joys and trials of motherhood, raising kids, and dealing with teenage problems.

In a short period of time, they quickly became podcasting stars, drawing hundreds of thousands of listeners and appearing on national news shows. Their show became so popular that Dixie Cup took notice and offered them a 12-month sponsorship deal worth over $100,000. All they had to do was mention Dixie Cup as their sponsor at the beginning and end of their Podcast. Imagine the possibilities advertising and the Internet can bring to your products or services!

You never know who is listening, watching, and willing to give you a huge paycheck for advertising. Big-name advertisers are now realizing that direct marketing and advertising via the Internet is more cost effective and reaches a broader audience than traditional methods and deliveries of advertisements.

Ten years ago, I never would have imagined being in the food business, considering I was a full-time Computer Sales Representative for a major corporation. My love of cooking led me to start my own personal chef and catering company, MishaCuisine.com.

Starting with just a business card and a website, I eventually expanded my services to include building a commercial kitchen. Realizing there was a need for Chefs and Caterers to have a facility to prepare their food services, I was able to meet that need and created an additional income stream in the process.

I realized that the secret to being a successful entrepreneur is that you have to constantly look for opportunities to grow.

Within a few years, my company has grown from an idea and a passion to cook to a full-fledged business. I also plan to expand my services to include online memberships and video recipes to teach people how to cook.

I accomplished my success by educating myself and using the tools and technologies available online. Everything starts with a simple idea. By taking action, the idea will become a reality.

Dreaming up of a business idea is easy. But taking it to a point where it starts to make sense and money requires time and dedication. Invest the required amount of time and needed dedication to make your business a success.

In my own experience, the most important foundation for success is actually very simple and often overlooked. Many people don't realize the power of having a business name, business checking account, and a business card. It's a state of mind and also a commitment to yourself. By taking the steps to establish your business identity, your ideas become real and, therefore, will begin to evolve and attract people that will help take your business to the next level.

I do different things on different days and sometimes 30 things in one day. Wearing many hats comes naturally because I love what I do; but most important of all, I know my limits. I know what I do best and how much I can do by myself, and I find support in others and their talents and gifts.

No one person can be good at everything; don't expect yourself to be. If you can recognize your strength and surround yourself with people who can complement your talents, you will be more successful.

Many of you have unique talents and skills, so have the courage to explore your ideas, even if it seems silly at the time. Don't let fear or criticism deter you from doing something for yourself. Don't wait for permission; just go for it.

Never limit yourself to just one business. Carry multiple business cards with you at all times. You never know what will take root!

Paulette Bethel

Paulette Bethel is a writer, editor and public speaker. As a student of metaphysics, Paulette has owned a bookstore, facilitated *A Course in Miracles*, had a successful counseling/rebirthing practice and edited the metaphysical newspaper, *Insights*. A long time animal lover, she co-founded a non-profit animal therapy organization for which she was Training Director for ten years. The book, *The Good Shepherd* by Jo Coudert, highlights the innovative therapeutic techniques Paulette helped develop. She hosted a two-hour talk radio show about animals. Currently, Paulette is a web designer and book editor. You can contact her by phone at (951)852-4808 or through her websites:

www.howtochooseapuppy.com
www.dobermans.net
www.proeditingservice.com

Chapter Nine

Slaying Dragons

Paulette Bethel

*E*ver since I can remember, I have been afraid! Afraid to try anything new, afraid of ridicule, afraid of making a mistake…the list is endless. I am one of those persons who really want to step up and step out, but my own dragons of fear have kept me restrained. You, too, may experience a debilitating fear of entrepreneurship.

If you are enterprising and fortunate, you may make a decision to start a business and just go for it. You would be in the minority, I believe. Most of us have to have a good prod with the proverbial poker in the rear end to get into doing something new and different. I had a wonderful mentor when I was a young woman, and she said the way to success lay in moving from inspiration rather than desperation.

Sounds easy, doesn't it? Well, let me tell you, it isn't! First of all, you will need to find a business to start. Do you have a passion in your life? Perhaps you love flowers and have a green thumb, or maybe you are a superb baker and your cakes are heavenly.

Examine your talents and interests and see if there isn't something you can do and do very well. That is a clue to doing something at which you can succeed. You need to be a self starter, as well.

Step 1: Find out what you are passionate about and can do well.

Step 2: Research the need for your service or product.

It is all well and good to love to grow flowers, but is there a need for that? You may be the most incredible creator of beautiful, tasty cakes; but if everyone you know or are around is on a diet, then cake isn't likely to be an easy path to success. However, if you have a means to market your cakes or flowers and a way to let those who want your service or products know you are available, then your immediate environment is not necessarily meaningful to the success of your business.

Step 3: Be open to expansion and possibilities that are connected to your enterprise.

For the sake of illustration, let's suppose you are gifted in the kitchen and you love to bake. You are creative in decorating cakes, and you have a talent for adding subtle flavors to your creations so that they are unique and in a class by themselves. So, you bake! And you sell.

Could you do more? Sure. How about teaching others some of the secrets of your trade, writing a newsletter that you sell on the Internet so others who want to know how you do it can learn? Or, maybe, you could hold classes on cake decorating. The list is really only as limited as your imagination. Who knows, you might even do a podcast on baking and decorating.

Step 4: Get educated in your chosen field.

Whether you are a butcher, a baker, or a candlestick maker, you are currently living in an amazing time of dynamic change. The Internet has made the entire world accessible. There are classes, even degrees that are available online.

Knowledge is still king, and it is easier and cheaper than ever before to avail yourself of it.

Step 5: Networking.

Find other individuals who are knowledgeable and working in your field of interest and exchange information.

It is possible to put a search phrase into 'Google' or 'Yahoo' and find thousands of others who have your same interests but with a slightly different bent. Those search engines can put you in touch with others who are bakers and cake decorators.

There are books to be found on how to do what you are already talented at doing, and those books were written by someone who has the same love of cooking that you do. Contact them. Start a blog on your chosen subject. Get the word out about you and your service.

Join an organization that has cake baking and decorating as a part of its purpose. Get out in the populace and participate in activities that expose your talents to the general public.

By all means, get a web site! That is a given in this day and age of Internet marketing. Make sure you are easy to find and reply to contacts.

What a wonderful time we live in! We can be driving across the country and sell a property using a cell phone and a fax machine, we can research property in a different state via the Internet, and we can do business without ever meeting a client face to face! You, too, may have done all of this at one time or another. I certainly have.

The only thing holding you back is yourself. If you are afraid, draw your sword and slay that fear dragon. If you don't know how to begin, keep on reading and make notes and take a chance!

There is a dragon of fear that has lived in my heart and resurrected itself repeatedly throughout my lifetime. That dragon has more lives than a cat, and I expect to go on slaying for many more years. Each time I do, I have that rush of accomplishment that is so fulfilling and makes life so sweet.

Has each of my ventures been successful? Yes! Have they all made money? Not all of them. But I learned from each experience and could apply that to the next attempt at 'fame and fortune'. In that sense, each enterprise was a huge success. I have found one of the best ways to learn something is to make a mistake. And then, go on to the next experience.

The only way we fail is if we give up. So far in my lifetime, I have been, among other things, a horse trainer, a dog trainer, a bookstore owner, an editor, an author, a public speaker, a talk radio host. I've been the subject of a 'How to' book on animal therapy and an advocate for small business enterprises.

I would sum up my chapter by saying there are a couple of things you need to do:

Make a list of what you love to do and think about a need for your particular passion or talent.

Pick one thing you do well.

Then, do some research to see if there is a need for your expertise. There has to be a demand or all the supply in the world will get you nowhere. Go to the Internet and avail yourself of one of the many 'How To' guides that are available; for instance, I suggest my personal favorite, www.homebusinesssuccesskit.com, and follow the steps that are outlined for doing the practical things; business cards, website, licenses, bank accounts, fictitious name announcements, and any other mundane thing you need to do to be a legitimate business. It will guide you, step-by-step, on how to set yourself up so others can find you, and you will benefit from the organized material that tells you how to get those necessary and oh so important items done.

Then, start slaying dragons. You can do anything you set your heart on if you believe you can. Create a treasure map and put on it those things that represent success to you. Surround yourself with people who are positive, loving, and supportive. Remember to give thanks for what you have and can do, even if it is only to get up in the morning and face another day. Focus on what you want and pursue it. If you have to, start with baby steps; eventually, those steps will become strides. The next thing you know, you will be wearing seven league boots and slaying dragons.

Find your passion and follow your dream, and you, too, will become an entrepreneurial woman.

Lina Mack Barker

Lina Mack Barker is an upcoming professional speaker and experienced woman entrepreneur, having owned and operated two successful floral shops in Southern California. She is also a chairperson for UCI Medical Center and has held that position for the past eight years. She currently consults in the medical industries helping her clients develop and operate their medical practices. Lina resides with her husband, Kelly Barker, in Southern California and loves being a grandmother to her three granddaughters, Brandy, Breanna, and Emillie, and one grandson, Brandon, as well as her husband's grandchildren. You can contact Lina Mack Barker at Lina@donboyer.org.

Chapter Ten

Mentoring a Child

Lina Mack Barker

*M*y children were always a tad resentful toward me when they were growing up because our house was continuously the temporary home for many strangers. People down and out on their luck came to live with us.

Even as a young newlywed, I felt the need to help others less fortunate than myself by allowing them to move into our home rent free, as long as they went to church with our family on Sunday and also attended our church's midweek service. Of course, these people had to either enroll in school or seek employment. Each person that lived with us was given six months to get their lives on the right track. I felt mentoring people would help them like I was helped early in my life.

I think I was about seventeen when I first realized that I was being mentored by a woman who was not my mother. Up until that time, I didn't have a clue what I wanted to do with my life. As a young girl, I don't even remember being asked what I wanted to be when I grew up.

I just took it for granted that I would grow up, get married, and my husband would take care of and be responsible for me—even if being married was not really what I wanted at the time. I never envisioned myself as a mom. Oh no, I was quite the big dreamer. I wanted to sing and dance on television. I wanted to be a Gold Digger on the Dean Martin Show, or sing on the Lawrence Welk Show, or be a comedy starlet on the Carol Burnett Show.

How could being on television be possible? I was one of ten children born to Mexican immigrants. My dad was a disabled veteran; my mom was a housewife, a very hard-working woman. Both of them didn't have much education; I think they went as far as the sixth grade. I don't think they had an idea how they would raise ten children. My parents certainly didn't have a manual to read or instructions to follow.

I am amazed at the amount of instruction given you when you buy almost anything. When I got my first television, the instruction manual for the remote control was two pages long. My car came with a leather-bound book, which told me about the engine and what the pretty little buttons on the dashboard were for. For example, the book explained how to operate the lights. You know, there are different kinds of lights, headlights, floodlights, emergency and indoor lights, as well.

Just think of all the stuff we get, both big and small, that comes with instructions. Yet, for the most important function in life, raising little people, we don't get a manual or any instructions. The doctors deliver these little people and hand them to us, not knowing us, our capacities or capabilities. We don't even have to take a test to be sure we are smart enough to handle the tremendous job of parenting.

When we bring this little person home, we tend to think that feeding and changing the baby is the hardest part of parenting. These new little humans are the blank books we parents get to write in. We get to help develop their personalities and their moral scruples.

That's right--no manual, no instructions. We fly by the seat of our pants for the most part. It's a whirlwind ride!

I thank God for my parents. Growing up, I remember thinking I would never be anything like those fogies. They were so hard to live with all their rules and regulations. Then it was my turn, and I was panic stricken. I grabbed all of my parents' rules and regulations because I wanted my children to grow up well balanced, happy, and, oh yes, good looking if at all possible. Of course, they would have to be thoughtful, caring, respectful, and loving. Would that be too much to ask for?

As my children started getting older, I remembered the most important ingredient to help me raise these little people—my spiritual values and foundation.

I am sure my children don't remember that day they no longer were babies. One day, they became strangers living in my house that liked talking back to me. They became disobedient and as mean to me as they could get away with. I was the person who had provided them with everything they needed in life up to that point in time. I had provided them with good shelter, shoes, and clothes. Maybe it was not everything they wanted, but I did the best I could.

How could this have happened? A famous newscaster once said, "What went wrong?"

Didn't they listen or remember the words of wisdom? Then, I received a glimpse of hope as I walked past my son's room and saw his Bible on his bed. Of course, I had to ask him, "Whose is that?" I was hoping to hear, "It's mine, Mom," which, thankfully, is what he said.

My youngest daughter, who is now a mother herself and is married to a wonderful man, called to ask me to stand in agreement with the things she desires. "Agree with me mom," she would say. I know she will do just fine in life because of the principles and wisdom I have instilled in her life.

I also have had the privilege of seeing what a wonderful mother my oldest daughter has become to her three children. She, too, is married to a wonderful man.

What? They were listening and have taken my advice, or at least some of it. Yes, one by one they grew up and became people of integrity, with good morals; they are kind, loving, caring people. I'm also happy to report they are good looking!

The funny part is, as they were growing up I thought they were supposed to be they only ones learning. I was the one teaching and mentoring them; they were to be the students and I was the teacher.

Much to my surprise, I learned so much, too. I learned unconditional love. I found that my children love me no matter what kind of parent I am or was to them. I learned that mentoring really does work. Here are four laws of mentorship:

Be an Example

We cannot lead one way and live another way; that is called hypocrisy. When our words and life are congruent, that is called integrity.

Believe in Yourself

You must believe in yourself before you can believe in others. What we teach and what we stand for is a reflection of what we have on the inside of us. To be an effective mentor and leader, you can only love and help people to the degree you love and help your self first.

Take Care of You

As mentors, many times we are always in the helping and serving mode, sometimes to the neglect of your own needs. Once again, we can only be effective to help people to the degree that we are taking care of ourselves. This includes our mental, physical, financial, relational, and business state. Mentoring people is a wonderful mission, but it requires that you stay in great shape.

Acceptance

One of the hardest things a true mentor faces is the realization that we cannot help some people, no matter how much we love them. Many times we want to help people more than they want to help themselves. You must remember, you are not the message, just the messenger. Trying to help and mentor those who are not interested in helping themselves is a road that leads to frustration and failure. You can give people the opportunity to help themselves but in the final analyses, it is their choice—not yours.

Gigi Simsiman

Gigi Simsiman and her husband, Dan, are co-founders of Wealthy Empowered Women, LLC-a seminar company; The Final Break Thru—a success coach company; and Power Me Now, Inc., a product line of Empowering Power Nap CDs. They are authors, professional public speakers, certified coaches and hypnotists who have assisted 15,000+ people in conquering their fears through exercises such as eating fire, breaking through boards and cement blocks, walking on glass, and jumping off 40' poles. Veterans of Corporate America, they chose to take their combined 40 years of experience and set themselves free as aspiring and inspiring entrepreneurs.

www.WealthyEmpoweredWomen.org
www.TheFinalBreakthru.com
www.PowerMeNowInc.org
gg@wealthyempoweredwomen.org
gg@thefinalbreakthru.com

Chapter Eleven

Empowered Women, *TAKE A STAND!!!*

Gigi Simsiman

*I*n this moment, we will look at several topics that will allow **Empowered Women to Take a Stand**! I have learned to master the topics, and they truly have made a difference in my life and allowed me to find my greatness within and maximize my potential! The empowering topics are described below.

1. Tithing and Philanthropy

Prior to my current success, my businesses did not succeed. The motivation, results, and financial rewards did not meet my expectations. It was painful. Until I learned about the ancient secret of tithing, I struggled to be successful.

In biblical times, Babylon was one of the richest nations because they tithed religiously. Abraham, Moses, and Joshua were millionaires during their time because of tithing. Even before then, Egyptian picture writing, cuneiform tablets, and the early writers of Rome and Greece prove that civilized nations practiced tithing as far back as 2000 B.C. As a matter of fact, it's been proven that tithing ten percent causes a tremendous increase in prosperity.

On February 26, 2005, I was given a Dream Sheet exercise to complete. The instructions are the foundation of the **7-Day Passion Technique**. As I was listening to the song that played, I wrote on my dream sheet: "I would like to build churches, missions, and soup kitchens in Third World Countries. I want to put clothes on people's backs, roofs over their heads, and food on the table. I do not want to feed them the fish, rather yet, I want to teach them how to fish." I later added to build schools and libraries after watching Oprah's dream come to fruition.

Since the day that I threw my ultimate dream and passion into the universe, everything started to align. People and resources appeared from out of the woodwork and flashed in front of me constantly. The universe and my creator have blessed me and continue to bless me with abundant people and resources!

I encourage you to visit my website and download my e-book. It will provide you with stories of what tithing and philanthropy has done for the wealthy. A few empowered women mentioned in the e-book are multi-billionaires because of the tithing and philanthropy that they have contributed to the world. A mentor taught me to do what the wealthy do, and in time I will be a mirror of these women.

I would like to add that you must *give* from your heart and do not *expect* anything back. Those who say that they do not have enough to tithe are the ones who must tithe now. Start tithing today. Start with 1% and increase it to 10% or more. You will be amazed at the blessings that immediately appear.

2. The 7-Day Passion Technique

The **7-Day Passion Technique** is what I came up with after hundreds of people confessed that they did not know what their passion was or how to find it. This technique works when you want it to work. When you find your passion, you will find the true essence of why you are here, as well as the gifts and talents you have to offer others.

- Play your inspirational song--a song that will be a positive mind trigger for you in this process.

- Find a quiet place and close the door.

- For **7 days, spend 30 to 45 minutes a day writing down** your passions, dreams, wants and desires. Do this at the same time of the day for the next **7 days** because the process ultimately becomes a mind trigger for you. Keep your head down, and let the writing flow. Do not analyze or critique your brain dump.

Do not concern yourself with spelling or grammar. Write in bullet-point format or even draw. Everyday, use a new piece of paper and do not re-read what was written the previous day.

- On the eighth day, gather and read all your sheets and find patterns in your writing. Find key words that repeat. You will find clarity in your writing during this process and open up portals to your subconscious. Many of your passions, dreams, wants, and desires have lain dormant in your subconscious because of human dream crushers in your life. This technique will bring them out into the surface.

- Extrapolate a page of affirmations based on any patterns you recognize. Start your affirmation with, "I am . . ." Hint: A habit forms every 21 days; therefore, every 30 days you should make and extrapolate a new page of affirmations.

- Make at least five copies of the affirmation page. Keep the original on your nightstand. Tape a copy in front of the toilet, bathroom mirror, refrigerator, kitchen sink, and in your car. Place one in your wallet or pocketbook. Type it into your laptop, PDA, or cell phone.

- After starting your day with love, joy, and happiness, reach over for the original and read it out loud. Throw it out into the universe. When you can read it out loud, act as if you are on the top of Mount Everest yelling down to the villagers so they can hear you. All five senses of your entire being should capture the emotion.

- Wherever you go, read your affirmations--read them everywhere at anytime!

- Record your affirmations with conviction, and play them over and over every night. When you record your affirmations, change "I am . . ." to "You are . . ."

By following this **7-Day Passion Technique**, you will find the passion that will move mountains, inspire and motivate you, and keep you focused on the ultimate plan. This process will also powerfully reprogram your subconscious, making you believe that you, too, are unstoppable!

3. Dream Board with Powerful Elements

Many teachers and avatars promote having a dream board in their books, workshops, and seminars. Dream boards are, indeed, important tools and sources of inspiration. However, several important elements are omitted in the instructions for putting a dream board together. Let's look at some of these elements and begin to incorporate them in your dream board.

First, I would like to say that putting a dream board together with pretty pictures is not enough. The dream board must have a powerful emotional charge for you. My first dream board had on it pretty pictures, for example, beautiful homes, cars, and jewelry. They were things I dreamed of obtaining, and they did not give me any emotional charge. So, I chose to do a new dream board. On my current board, I have pictures of children from Third World Countries, non-profit organizations, and philanthropic mentors. Now when I look at my dream board, beyond the children's eyes, I see the suffering that they are going through. To this day, my dream board makes me cry, and that is my emotional charge. Do you feel the intention and emotional charge?

Next, when you put your dream board together, make sure the pictures are administered in proper Feng Shui. For more insight on Feng Shui, go to our website and click on Feng Shui with Iris. Iris incorporates the essence of Feng Shui to dream boards, such as the importance of the relationship corner or prosperity corner.

Finally, strategically place your dream board in your bedroom directly across the line of sight where you first wake up every morning. For example, I tend to wake up on my side facing the wall. My dream board is pinned up against that wall on its side so I may properly read the words on the board even though my head is still on my pillow. And what better way to begin my day with these motivating and inspiring pictures!

4. Take Action Now!

> Thinking, Thinking, Thinking . . .
> Planning, Planning, Planning . . .
> Researching, Researching, Researching . . .
> Preparing, Preparing, Preparing . . .

Enough already! All are necessary tasks that we can agree on. And unless you put all of it into **ACTION**, all of the above does you no good. Take the first step to your new endeavor or process, and the second step will be revealed. Fail forward fast! In every mistake, there is a blessing. Quickly make all the mistakes you can and learn from your blessings. Understand that the correct path or process will appear at the right time. Master what you are good at doing. Always ask yourself "What is the highest and best use of my time?" Whatever is painful and time consuming for you to do, realize there is another who was blessed with the talents and abilities that you lack. Search for the right person to do the job.

5. Capitalize by Dovetailing Multiple Streams of Income

Dovetailing is a very important concept for any empowered entrepreneur to understand. The empowered entrepreneur should utilize this strategy to capitalize on all they can in the marketplace. For example, let's say that you are a real estate investor. Beyond simply investing in real estate, the real estate investor can write a book on investing, speak at a real estate workshop or seminar, sell their products or services on the internet, or be a network marketer selling related products. In addition, when coaching and mentoring on real estate investing, you may offer life and success coaching, teleseminars, webinars, or provide monthly newsletters. This is the concept of dovetailing; it allows you to cover all your bases when building your business. It allows you to play every ace to maximize your potential income. Successful entrepreneurs use this concept constantly. When you attend the next Empowered Women Take A Stand Seminar, you will learn how to masterfully dovetail multiple streams of income into your business.

6. Be a Masterful Closer

Repeat after me...

"I am a Master Closer! I love to close!"

"I love to close my products and services!"

"I have an obligation to close my products and services because it will make a difference in my client's life!"

Understand that there is a science behind closing. Believe that you have a strong ability to close and command a sale. There are many books and seminars in the market. I suggest that you invest in many books and seminars to fine-tune your ability to close on sales. The seminars and books I've invested in have taught me the science of persuasion and influence. I have incorporated this science to become and act as though "I am a Master Closer!" I am now seen in the seminar industry as a leader and an example of the ability to close and command a sale. You, too, can achieve this.

Become a salesperson and realize that eventually you have to sell the number one product to everyone to become successful, and the number one product is yourself!

7. Forever Be a Student and Continue to Gain More Knowledge

Forever be a student and when it is time to be the teacher, be a teacher-student. Always be in the learning mode. As you teach your student, employee, or even yourself, always ask how you can be better.

Let me give you an example. After a seminar, a coaching session, or a specific task, I suggest sitting down to complete an "After Action Review." The questions on the review are as follows:

- What worked well?
- What could have been better or improved?
- What empowered you?

Asking these questions will allow opportunities for you, the student, to improve yourself and to gain more knowledge. Know that applied knowledge is power. And remember, by asking the final question, "What empowered you?," you will end the review on a positive note and it will become a mind trigger to projected future success!

8. Have a Coach Who Practices Subconscious Reprogramming

Surround yourself with like-minded people. Your coach should be like-minded, as well. Invest in a coach or mentor who practices subconscious reprogramming. There will be times in which you may be challenged, unexpected issues and problems may arise, fears and doubts might hit you like a ton of bricks. Your coach must have resources and tools to pull you out of any challenge in the way of accomplishing your dreams and passions. You will need a powerful, results-oriented coach who is aware of your mind triggers and has the ability to get you back to the positive emotional state that keeps you productive. Log on to my website and receive a Free Daily Empowerment Positive Affirmation from Power Me Now as a special gift.

9. Prayer, Meditation, and Gratitude

Always, always be grateful. I was once told, "We all were blessed with gifts, talents, and abilities, and our gift is what we do with the gifts, talents, and abilities that were given to us." I always set aside time to pray or meditate in the morning and at night. I found that I continue to receive more and more blessings because I take the time to be grateful for the blessings that I've been given. Trust me, do the same, and abundance will flow continually into your hands!

To find out more about the nine concepts and receive a monthly newsletter, visit our websites:

www.EmpoweredWomenTakeAStand.com
www.TheFinalBreakthru.com

God Bless You and All of Your Endeavors.

Happy, Happy, Joy, Joy.

Warmly, Gigi Simsiman

Lisa Mason DiSalvio

Lisa Mason DiSalvio left her position as a speech pathologist after she and her husband, Stephen, launched Cornerstone Real Estate Investors, LLC. They have traveled extensively to pursue their journey of self-development, and this journey has inspired them to want to share their experiences and knowledge with others. To this end, they have started a new company called Firestarters, which strives to reach people through personal coaching and speaking events. Lisa and Stephen have been mentored in real estate by Jon and Stephanie Iannotti, are graduates of Greg Pinneo's Power Players program, The Bridge with Life Tigers and the Present with Purpose program with George Ramirez.

Contact Lisa at:
lisadisalvio@yahoo.com
304-905-0936

Chapter Twelve

Making the Pieces
of the Puzzle Fit

Lisa Mason DiSalvio

*W*hen I was a young girl, I loved Christmas. I loved everything about it--the lights, the tree, the music, visiting family (which always meant chips, dip and great cookies!!), the shopping, and well, I loved the presents, too. One day, I decided I wanted to design a new Christmas decoration. As I sat on my bed imagining what it could be, I envisioned icicle lights. Yes, icicle lights. When I shared the idea with someone, I was told it couldn't be done. Well, someone else had that same idea. That someone designed them a little differently than my young mind did, but they designed them, and now you can't ride down a street at Christmas and not see them – icicle lights.

What's your dream? What lurks inside of you, in the unspoken corners of your heart and soul? What do you think can't be done? Or can be done, but not by you?

Imagine with me now building a jigsaw puzzle. Have you ever been building one and as the picture begins to take shape, you get stuck and you can't seem to make another piece fit? Then, you realize that a piece has dropped on the floor, you pick it up, put it in place, and on you go. I have found this to be a great analogy for my life.

Over my childhood and teenage years, many pieces were added to my puzzle box by many wonderful people. And, well, a few added some pieces that needed to be sorted out and thrown away. For many years of my adult life, all of these pieces lay scrambled inside of the box, i.e., inside of me. Occasionally something or someone would shake that box and a few pieces dropped out, but no picture was started, not even the frame. At least, not the picture that I held in my heart.

One time, several years ago, I was in the midst of a break-up of a significant relationship and was struggling to make my way through the fog. I walked into the office of a co-worker one day, and she was talking about someone named "Paul" who had left his position with his company and opened his own private practice as a counselor. I inquired further about Paul and decided he sounded like someone who could help me through what I was experiencing. As it turned out, the relationship was a minor part of what we discussed. The things that Paul was able to help me see about myself were amazing. It was a time when I learned to treat myself well. I learned that I could be a good and loving person and still take good care of me. I learned to start freeing my spirit and to start valuing myself. I learned to treasure my time with my female friends and that I didn't have to measure the goodness of something by whether or not it involved meeting a guy. (Of course now that I'm married, I really value time with my female friends, and I don't want any men to be there!!) I began to learn that it is okay to reach for more. I learned that I could love my parents without being like my parents and that they would always love me regardless of my choices. I learned the journey truly is the destination. I learned to start shedding baggage (why is it that when I fly, the airline never loses that baggage?). I learned I could forgive. And, through this experience, the outside frame of my puzzle was created. I could see a new picture of my life unfolding.

Unfortunately, the core of the picture was based on decisions I had made previous to this experience. The new frame was my new life. The core pieces were from my old life. I still knew, deep in my heart and soul, that I wanted more, could be more, could do more, and could live a life that made a difference to me and to the world.

I found my answer in owning my own business. My husband and I first launched a real estate investing business; this changed my life and a whole new learning experience was started. Owning our own business brought with it necessary changes. I learned to talk to people whether I knew them or not, and I learned to be the first one to smile and say hi.

Everyday something requires me to move out of my comfort zone. I gained a new self-confidence and finally started to live the life I wanted, not the life I thought others wanted for me. I learned to seize the "opportunities of a lifetime" instead of passing them by, sometimes not knowing exactly why I was doing it or even how. I learned to stretch my tolerance for risk. Again, I learned that the journey truly is the destination. By owning our own business and taking control of our lives and our destinies, I now live enjoying the journey and no longer feel like something's missing from my life. Most importantly, I learned that life can be good and it can be all I want it to be.

And so my journey continues into even greater experiences. Throughout these phases of my personal development, a dream that lurked in the corners of my heart was being able to one day share all I had learned in order to help others change their lives, too. My husband and I have started a second company called "Firestarters." We created the name based on a quote from a French General in World War I, Ferdinand Foch, who once said, "There is no greater weapon on earth than the human soul on fire." Both my husband and I have had our souls set on fire, and we want to help others to do the same. Our goal is to help people pursue their own self-development and to coach people in all walks of life to give value to their dreams and to find a way to live that dream.

Remember, it started with a break-up, a door closed, and a very tentative young woman tip-toeing through the next door. And now, I look with great anticipation for the next open door that I can run through at full speed. I live with great excitement about what the next piece of my puzzle will be.

Lessons along life's journey do not always come easy. There were a number of people, activities, and changes in thought processes that helped me along the way. The following is a list of some of the most important ways that I found to make this journey a successful one.

Prayer: One of the greatest lessons for me in terms of prayer was that the small, still voice in my heart was God's way of communicating with me. For many years, I didn't value that voice because I didn't understand what it was. I learned to trust and to honor that voice.

Daily motivational input: I have many ways of getting my daily dose of motivational input. I listen to, read, or watch something inspirational everyday. I have favorite books and favorite CDs. I found the important key here is to do it everyday. Without the daily input, it is easy to return to old habits and old thought patterns. The daily input keeps me going in the direction I desire.

Finding GREAT mentors: I have had, and will continue to have, not just one, but many great mentors; they all have something of tremendous value to offer and teach me; and then my role is being the best student possible and sharing what I have learned with others.

Making decisions regarding life experiences: Whatever good I experience in life, I choose to take along with me; and as for the bad experiences, I choose to no longer let them define me.

Taking control of my thoughts: I remember everyday how much of my life I create by what and how I am thinking; I practice the Law of Attraction

Taking risks: This was a huge part of my transition, as I had not in earlier years learned to be a risk taker; I started with small risks, found out I survived and then took bigger risks. I still have a few more risks in my future!!

Now my puzzle is growing. Good experiences and great mentors, family and friends have helped me to pick up the pieces that fell to the floor so I can continue building my puzzle. I realize now that for many years I was a victim—a victim of many negative thought processes that created a limited belief system.

What are you a victim of? Is it negative thinking, bad experiences, comfort zone, fear, others' expectations or something else? Make a list of yours, and then remember, there are two words that begin the same, but end very differently. They are: VIC-TOR and VIC-TIM. Our lives all start the same, and it is up to us how they end. I will continue to add pieces to my puzzle until my last breath is taken. And then, my puzzle won't be one picture, it will be several pictures of Lisa, the entrepreneur, the author, the motivational speaker, the wife, the daughter, the friend, the philanthropist, the mentor AND the student, the adventurer, and many more. These pictures will all be surrounding one word......VICTOR.

How do you want to spend your life.........what will your ending be?

Charlotte Newbert

Charlotte Newbert is the director of Newbert Revolution, Ltd, a company set up to manufacture and distribute Jade based beauty products, such as the Nephria Jade Beauty Bar. Her story is an inspiration for other women. Following an idyllic childhood in northern England, she evolved into a studious and dedicated student of business. Then, she settled in the culturally diverse and exciting city of Manchester, where she was involved in an insurance partnership. As her business interests developed, she sought more of a challenging lifestyle. Having been a regular worldwide traveler, she discovered an amazing beauty range whilst in South Korea, and the remainder of her story is her own little piece of history. She confidently declares that she loves every minute of her new venture, with her husband and partner in all respects, Andrew, and the thrill of being her own boss at last is immense. Charlotte may be contacted at:

www.newbertrevolution.com
Email: charlotte@nephria.com

Chapter Thirteen

Follow Your Dream

Charlotte Newbert

I am a 40 year old professional, who gave up a 15 year career as a partner in a major insurance practice and moved to the South Coast of England to sell soap. So many people said, "She is so brave to be giving up a nice life," or "Charlotte is now selling soap; I can't see that working." The patronizing smiles and negative comments just made me even more determined. I don't think there are many people in my circle who would have believed my achievements to date. While it is very empowering to prove the naysayers wrong, it is vitally important to be pulled by your own passion, not pushed by other people's negative observations. While the push of your detractors will fade, the pull of your own determination will only increase.

My name is Charlotte Newbert, and this is a story about my business. I have had so many exciting things happen to me in 2007 which I never imagined or dreamed possible. It is amazing what we, as females, are actually capable of.

I now have sole worldwide distribution rights for my product, which has been featured in many magazines, both here and abroad. It has been featured in the Billionaires Shopping List in Stuff Magazine and magazines in Marbella, Barbados, U.K., America, and Moscow. I have also been interviewed on T.V. and radio. My product will be featured in a book called *Toys for Girls*, due to be released in September, 2007. *Toys for Girls* includes the most prestigious and luxurious products in the world, is published in three languages and distributed worldwide.

I am the director of Newbert Revolution, Ltd. – the company I set up after traveling to Korea and finding the Nephria Jade Beauty Bar.

As I approached midlife, I began to feel more and more unfulfilled and bored in my career. Monetary and creature comforts and big city living were no longer enough. I knew I wanted to leave the hustle and bustle of city life for something different, and the thought of a life by the sea became appealing. I found a fantastic and unique product, and I knew it from my gut reaction. Nothing was going to stand in my way.

With all the bureaucratic interference and government meddling in the world of insurance, coupled with having to work with some very wealthy, yet remarkably demanding, people, I knew I needed an alternative. For several months, I toyed with starting my own little empire; and through a chance meeting on holiday in Korea, I now have a sole worldwide distribution agreement to market and sell an amazing, unique, and totally individual product.

I am fantastically proud of my change in life and direction and love sharing my experiences with you. I attended business seminars, leadership and management days, and sought financial and investment advice. When one has many years of experience in any mainstream business line, you rely on your common sense, experience, and the information available. I have become a prolific reader of self-help and advice books, in addition to referring to the huge amount of information freely available on the Internet.

In regard to the risks, if you don't try, you will never know. At times, I occasionally harbor these thoughts, but only for a moment, because I really believe I am now in charge of my own future. The boring regional meetings and clients I knew before Christmas seem like distant memories.

Anything is possible if you have a good idea, good product, good work ethic, and the ability to work toward your own targets and limits. Those who might view this as too risky should stay in the Rat Race and let the visionaries try their hand in other entrepreneurial lines. I tried, and I'm glad I did.

I was inspired by one particular A-Ha moment and a desire for something better, fueled by successful friends and acquaintances, each of whom said that there is more to life than being unfulfilled. I was unfulfilled in my career in the insurance industry, where I'd been for 15 years. I wanted the freedom to make my own decisions and to be the master of my own destiny.

Driven by curiosity, motivation, and stimulation, I began to look at the world of business and commerce. I needed to find a wealth-generating scheme that would reward me for my application, effort, and intellect, rather than for a unique talent or ability. Among many areas of interest, the theme that came back time and time again was the world of trade and import/export. It is an area of business that requires application, procedural and regulatory knowledge, and commitment, but was advantageous to me for the following reasons:

- I was prepared to do anything that was within our own perspective of decency.

- I was totally mobile and flexible.

- I considered myself to be trainable, a fast learner, and quick on the uptake.

- I was open to almost any area of business, commerce, and supply.

Having stumbled upon the concept of being an import and export agency, I began to research how the world of trade worked. Within reason, it is not complicated; and I was also well aware after a significant amount of travel that there are some fantastic products overseas that we do not have at home.

There is so much out there that is being bought and sold at any given moment. The skill of the expert agent is to notice what is wanted and find a place to supply it.

During my research and travels, I was most fortunate to make the acquaintance of a manufacturer and production engineer who has since become my main supplier. I now have a long-term worldwide distribution agency agreement with him.

The naughts are the women born of the last generation of mums and housewives. Having been educated in the 1970's and 1980's, I am of the generation of women who have been empowered with the education, worldliness (through travel, business experience, and the late 20th century information explosion) to be convinced that the stereotypical organic family of my youth is not the most effective use of the brain in my skull.

As I move into my forties, I've never felt as powerful, influential, and recognized as I do now. I believe it is this decade that will see the end of the Victorian model of family life. I also think many women are starting businesses for the freedom that it brings, allowing those who set up home businesses to be there for their families.

I am anxious to heed the advice of people who are where I want to be. I also learn from books, the Internet, newspaper articles, and my gut instinct, which has been right for me more times than you could imagine. As my business network expands, I expect to listen and learn from people in positions of influence, but I have not yet found that to be necessary or always easy to arrange.

Consider being an entrepreneur if you are hungry for knowledge and monetary success, and enjoy the fear and excitement of uncertainty. Be prepared to be tired, worried, up early, in bed late, to lose contact with acquaintances because Saturday night in the pub is no longer appealing, and you would rather fly to Glasgow for a trade fair than go to the theatre in London. If you agree with my thoughts, become an entrepreneur—you certainly have it in you.

I hope my story is an inspiration to other women to start their own companies.

It is hard, and it does take time; but I truly believe that once we put our mind to it, have faith and believe in ourselves, we are capable of much more than we ever dreamed.

If you think you can, you can; if you think you can't, you can't.

Olivia D. Ramirez

Olivia D. Ramirez is a very accomplished educator with several credentials. Her love is working with Kindergarten children. With over 30 years experience in this field, her impact on many lives is quite amazing. Although she has traveled to over 20 countries throughout the world with her husband, George, her newest and greatest adventure is being a grandmother to Alisha, (nicknamed "Sunshine"). Olivia's message of encouragement and taking control is for everyone. Olivia can be contacted by telephone at 1-866-945-4730 or by sending an email to gopassiton@yahoo.com.

Chapter Fourteen

Wealth... Without Health?
Using the Law of Attraction for Your Health

Olivia Ramirez

*A*s I have grown as a person, I've noticed just how many reasons there are for being balanced in my life. One point that really stands out is how often people compromise their health as they pursue wealth.

I realize that when one is 25 years old and invincible, health-related issues aren't even considered. But as life moves on, being able to fully enjoy what one has been blessed with becomes a more prominent concern. Of course, everyone wants to live to be 120 years old! But not if they're hooked up to some machine and strapped into a bed with no real mobility. We desire a free, vibrant, and exciting life...right?

I know a couple. I'll call them Fred and Alice, (yes, just like the honeymooners); they have been married for many, many years and are still very much in love. They were both successful in business, raised wonderful children, have money to spend, a beautiful hilltop home and even some grandchildren to enjoy.

All was well and going according to plan until about five years ago when Alice started to slip, fall, and drop things. Fred cared for her; there were two major surgeries that produced no positive results. Fred hired live-in help so that he could continue tending to business.

One day while on a small stepladder at home, he grew dizzy and fell. He hit his head and lay bleeding for over two hours until help arrived. He recovered, but the dizziness came back and got worse. He had trouble driving; soon he was spending several days at a time in hospital care. He suffered from dementia, then a stroke.

After a slight recovery, both he and his wife are in separate facilities, each needing 24-hour care. They ask, but can rarely see each other.

This is robbery! Robbed of time and experiences that could be spent with family and friends.

Does any of this sound familiar to you? You may know others in a similar situation. What if it were you? What if illness were keeping you from enjoying the fruits of your labor?

Well, I am here to tell you that you can keep your health and enjoy an abundant life!

After seeing the movie *The Secret*, reading the book and attending the movie premier of *Pass It On* (my husband is actually a costar and associate producer in the movie), I know the time is right for me to share my story.

W I S H is not only the name of the company that produced the movie; it is also an acronym for what the movie is about. Wealth, Inspiration, Success, Happiness...Both *The Secret* and *Pass It On* stress the power of our thoughts and words.

I was reacquainted with how to use the Law of Attraction after seeing the movies.

You see, over 20 years ago, I had learned about the Law of Attraction. It was back then that my study and research began. It is basically the same concept, the power of our thoughts and words over our health and circumstances.

I used it specifically for health, here is what happened...

During a routine female exam, my gynecologist took a sonogram and discovered three cysts that, when combined, were the size of a man's wallet. He recommended surgery.

I asked if timing was critical and if the surgery could be delayed for a while. He said yes, it could be delayed, and that is when I went to work. I used the Law of Attraction with scriptures, my words, affirmations, and visualization.

One year later, I returned. The three cysts were now pinhead size! And I had suffered no ill or side effects.

Here is what I did:

1. FORGIVENESS:

It's a good thing that I have always been quick to forgive. But, I searched my heart honestly and thoroughly, anyway. I checked my emotions for hurt feelings. Even simple hurts needed to be eliminated or guarded against. Remember, forgiveness does you more good than it does for the one you forgave.

2. ASK:

"We have not, because we ask not." So I asked... I asked that "the cysts shrink to nothing." It was a clear, specific request with the desired results spoken in the form of a declaration.

This is an important point; my husband and I spoke about this plan, and we agreed on the desired results. We were in unity. We watched our words and were in total harmony. Now, the power of agreement was also at work.

3. BELIEVE:

I chose to believe that I had what I had asked for. I didn't allow myself to dwell on any thoughts of unbelief or doubt. Those thoughts will always come up; you must forcibly push them aside and replace them with thoughts of the desired results. I treated these thoughts as trash. I would visualize myself ripping these pages out of the tablets of my mind, and I then would crush the pages and throw them into the trash can. The more I did this, the more I aligned myself with my healing. You will have to decide on what you want. It is always a choice!

I used daily affirmations. Included were my scriptures that I prefaced with "I believe...." or "It is written...:" Each affirmation ended with the desired result.

4) RECEIVE:

I chose to not talk about the problem. I chose to think on the results as though they were in the present tense, NOW!

Be thankful. It is called gratitude! As I visualized the cysts shrinking this caused the emotion of gratitude to rise up. I definitely had the "Attitude of Gratitude" for the miracle that had taken place in my body. I had already received my healing. I was just waiting for my body to catch up with my beliefs and emotions.

When you truly believe you receive something, you ACT LIKE IT! So, I did. A cheery heart is good medicine, so like my friend Greg Reid, a.k.a. The Millionaire Mentor, always says, "Keep Smilin."

The final sonogram report of the shrunken cysts was just icing on the cake.

Finally, I want this writing to be an encouragement. I wish it to instill faith and hope in you. Use it to keep or regain your health, the Law of Attraction will help you either way.

I am a grandmother that enjoys a vibrant active life. I can be completely involved in our grandchild's life. Her name is Alisha; we lovingly call her "Sunshine".

No limitations! Do the things you know, like eat good food, work out, rest, and avoid stress.

But, always include a daily dose of Forgiveness, Asking, Believing and Receiving.

It worked for me; I believe it will work for you.

Melissa Day

Melissa Day has always had an entrepreneurial spirit. In 1990, she obtained a degree from the USC Business Entrepreneur School and focused on Marketing and Real Estate. Since then, Melissa has brought creative and skilled marketing magic into her ventures. A successful Real Estate Investment Consultant, Melissa's mission is to *"Help You Invest in Your Future!"* She utilizes **streaming media technology,** where success is measured with <u>results</u>. Melissa is considered an expert with a cutting edge in today's real estate market. She offers Internet-based marketing solutions and trains her investment clients and associates to become masters of their own marketing and create their own magic. You can reach Melissa directly at (619) 922-1857 or info@melissadayinvesting.com.

"I would like to dedicate this chapter to my mother, Donna Louise Day. She was my very first mentor and instilled in me the belief that I could do and be <u>anything</u>. It is because of my mother that I have a desire to pursue my dreams and the belief and certainty that I will succeed. Thank you, Mom…because of you, I am living my passion!" ~ Melissa

Chapter Fifteen

Apply the Wisdom of Your Mentors With the Right Attitude

Melissa Day

J'm not going to share with you a story where I have suffered, struggled, and overcome insurmountable obstacles to become a success. My story is more typical. It is just a story of life's usual challenges, with one major difference...

ATTITUDE!

By living with an *attitude of gratitude*, my journey has been one that focuses on appreciation for all that I have, all that I encounter (including the challenges), and everyone I meet. The principles you learn from your mentors are more effective if you have the right attitude, so it makes sense to come from a place of gratitude. I have found that if you come from this place of gratitude any time you are experiencing adversity, then you find strength in your appreciation and can overcome them more easily.

Challenges <u>shape</u> *you.*
Attitude <u>defines</u> *who you are.*

The most difficult challenge of my life was losing my mother in 1997. Her death was sudden, and it shook me to the core. But I chose to move forward because I knew that my mother would want me to continue the search for my life purpose...my passion. She always told me..."*If you can find a way to save people <u>time</u>, you will be a millionaire!*" I never forgot this little gem—and as I pursued my passion—her words resonated with me.

During this time, I was running my own personal training business and by helping people achieve their fitness goals, I was truly connected to something I felt passionate about. But there was something missing. My life did not feel balanced. I decided to make a change and continued the search for the missing piece—the piece that would complete my passion, rather than just feed one part of it. Because of my tenacity, I was able to solve Mom's puzzle! The solution to *saving people time* was not apparent at first; but once I discovered it, I knew that I had found my true passion—which was helping people grow and prosper in their investments and businesses. I offer solutions for investors and business owners that DO save them time and even better, saves them money, as well, via streaming media marketing.

What does being an entrepreneur mean for a woman?
Being in charge of your own destiny!

What a wonderful feeling! You are empowered and excited about this amazing journey, right? And at times, you may also feel scared and uncertain. It is part of the ride, so hang on…and embrace it!

I have always had an entrepreneurial spirit. It is an energy that drives me. Since I have experienced both failure and success as an entrepreneur in a variety of ventures, I want to share with you what I feel are the key components to being a successful business owner. I hope to inspire you and spark something in you so that you realize your dreams and enjoy the amazing freedom that being an entrepreneur offers.

Passion ~ Intention ~ Focus ~ Balance
Finding Your Passion!

Imagine waking up each day feeling excited and eager about what you are going to accomplish. Your mind is active the minute you awake, and you leap out of bed ready to seize the new day. Sounds like a great way to live, doesn't it? Well, if you do what you are *passionate* about – this is how every day will start. Finding your passion is essential to being a successful business owner. Let's face it, as women, we are passionate by nature! We put our heart and soul into whatever we are passionate about. We are unstoppable when we are armed with this enthusiasm! Passion is so important, especially for women because to be a successful entrepreneur, you must call upon every ounce of your <u>inner strength</u> to stay on track, and this strength is fueled by your passion.

Another truth about women is that when we believe in something so intensely, we invest our whole being. When we do not believe in something, then we do not give the same amount of energy and commitment to it. Your business will need an intense commitment for it to thrive.

Take a moment to think about your passion. Do you already know what you are passionate about? If you haven't felt an incredible driving force propelling you forward, it's time to find your passion right now! Take out a piece of paper and pen and get ready to do a free-flowing brainstorm.

➔ Write down at least 10 activities that you absolutely LOVE to do. Don't hold back. Don't make judgments or criticisms of yourself for loving these activities. Just write them down now.

➔ Next, list at least 2-3 skills that you possess that compliment each of these activities.

➔ Look at your list. Close your eyes and think about what NEED exists in the world *already* that could be filled with any one or any combination of these activities and skills.

Now, for the fun part...

➔ Don't stop there. Dig deep! What product or service could you offer that *creates a need* that you can ultimately fill? Let your creativity flow... without judgment.

What is your WHY?

Once you truly know what your *whys* are, you will be even more connected to your passion and you'll have more reasons and feelings to support it.

Answer these questions to discover your *whys*:

- What do you want to SEE in the world?
- What do you want to POSSESS for pure pleasure?
- What do you want to EXPERIENCE and with whom?
- What MESSAGE do you want to impart to others?
- What IMPACT do you want to make in the world?
- What or how do you want to GIVE BACK?

So…think about *your whys* and write them down so you can get more connected with your passion.

Setting Your Daily Intention

By setting your intention <u>every day</u>, you empower yourself to achieve exactly what you desire for your life. If you skip this important step, then you may easily get distracted and head in the wrong direction.

Intention is tricky because it is not something you DO; rather it manifests as a thought, and then becomes an energy that you put out into the world. As we know from *The Secret*, which teaches us about **The Law of Attraction,** *thought becomes reality.*

<u>Start Simple and Be Specific!</u>

Intention is about AWARENESS. When you choose your intention each day, you are telling yourself and the universe that <u>you want to be aware</u> of this specific need or goal.

Why is intention important for a woman entrepreneur?

We are beings that are queens of multitasking. This is one of our most esteemed attributes! But, it can mean that we end up *reacting* to everything that we encounter and fail to accomplish the integral tasks that will get us closer to our goal. By setting your intention each day, you are sure to attract (be more aware of) exactly what you need/want to accomplish that day.

Intention allows you to be in the moment while driving forward toward your goals.

Get into a routine of setting your intention *every* morning. You can do this as you wake – as you open your eyes, during a morning meditation, while you are exercising or as you have breakfast. The key is to set your intention in the <u>morning</u>! **Every morning!** Start simple. For example, state, *"I will remember to take a deep breath every time I feel pressured or stressed."*

Get a feel for how your awareness changes as you become more disciplined at setting your intention – and tuning into it throughout the day. You'll find that the results you see from your day that *begins with intention* are more incredible than those without intention. Believe it or not…women can accomplish <u>even more</u> than we ever thought possible with the powerful tool of intention.

Sharpening Your Focus

This practice goes hand-in-hand with setting your intention. Focus is the most important ingredient to staying on course. Without focus, you are like a sailboat in the middle of the big blue sea, without a chart, compass, or GPS! How do you navigate the waters, especially when the inevitable storm comes?

Setting our focus is especially difficult for women because we want to *accomplish it all*. We feel confident and proud about our ability to multitask, so we courageously step up to the plate and declare, *"We can do it all!"*

But wait! Can you really do it all…and do it all *well?* Having a sharp focus is the key to achieving results. Once you hone in on this skill, you will be more powerful as a woman business owner and will even surprise yourself at what you can accomplish!

Where do you start? You have numerous tasks, ideas and goals swimming in your head. Focus is actually easier than you think! Below are a few core points to help you sharpen your focus:

1) **Pinpoint your natural talents and your strengths.** *Write them down and embrace them! Recognize yourself for having these talents!*

   As you focus on your natural talents and strengths, notice that you can delegate the tasks and activities that you are not as good at to someone else. This will free up time for you to focus on what you do well.

2) **Identify bad habits and take steps to change them into more successful habits.** *For every bad habit – write down a more successful habit that can replace it.*

   Once you identify your bad habits and take the steps to change them into more productive and successful habits, you will eliminate wasted energy and start to realize your true potential.

3) **Look at the big picture!**

   By taking time to focus on the big picture, you will aim your goals so that they all point toward your ultimate desires – your passions! You will have more clarity so that you can develop a solid plan that will bring you closer to your goals.

4) **Create *optimum balance* for your life.**

   I feel that this should be a primary goal for every woman.

   But note…balance is always changing as you move throughout life. Be ready for fluctuations…and accept them. True balance is in a constant state of change…so get ready for the ride! *(We'll discuss this more in the next section!)*

Maintaining Your Balance

What does balance mean to you? This concept is actually different for everyone. We all have an innate need for balance, but many of us are oblivious to this need. Life just *happens,* and we ignore the signs from our body, our minds, our hearts – and even our mentors…that tell us that we are out of balance!

Balance = Peace

Since balance is constantly *changing,* can we ever be at peace and remain at peace? **Yes, we can!** Because once we know what aspects of life are part of our balance, we can *allow* the natural fluctuation…*accept* the changes…and *embrace* the flow of life!

The primary components of balance are:
Career/Financial
Health/Fitness
Spirituality
Relationships

Each of these has a level of importance in your life. It is up to you to determine what amount of importance each part holds. You may not have considered the role balance played in your life before, but perhaps felt at times that something was "out of whack." This unsettled feeling is the universe letting you know that your life is not in balance. Once you become aware of how each element fits into <u>your</u> life, you will naturally strive to maintain your balance. Sometimes it will take a conscious effort, and other times it will just come naturally. As you consider each component, think about how each one fits into your idea of a balanced life.

Career/Financial…

How do you feel about your career? Do you like what you are doing? Do you feel successful? Have you accomplished your career goals? Are you looking to make a change…and perhaps been putting it off? How do you feel about the level of income you are making? Are you satisfied with your income or do you want to earn more money? Ultimately – what is going to make you feel happy and fulfilled (and passionate) about your career and financial success?

Health/Fitness...

What does good health mean to you? Does it mean good physical condition? Does it mean feeling energized and strong inside? Perhaps it means that you get a clean bill of health at your annual physical. Whatever your definition of good health/fitness is, this is your <u>foundation</u> that you will build upon. What level of health/fitness will make you feel vital and alive?

Spirituality...

Everyone has a different spiritual inspiration and focus. It is essential to your balance to tap into what your true spiritual connection is. For some people, this is very easy because they have always been in tune with their spirituality. For others, it is more difficult because they have not tapped into this part of their life. Your spirituality is your inner strength. This is your connection to a *higher power* that you call upon when you encounter challenges, fears, and obstacles. This inner strength is what empowers you to tackle the challenges, defeat the fears, and overcome the obstacles.

Draw on your spirituality for this strength! Prayer and meditation are techniques many people use to connect to their spiritual source. What is yours?

Relationships...

This is a critical topic for women, because we tend to invest our entire being into our relationships. Whether it is family, friends, or a romantic relationship – we give our whole self to this important component. **Women are givers!** The danger in this is that we often pull ourselves out of balance because we put too much focus on this one area. The other areas of our lives can actually suffer because we may not even realize our balance is so skewed until we become aware that the other areas are lacking. Usually – when this occurs – we are so far out of balance that it is difficult to regain control…and often, the relationships suffer, too. Take a look at the significant relationships in your life now and assess their impact and influence on your life. Do you feel that these relationships are empowering and fulfilling, or are they draining and frustrating? As you assess your relationships, decide where they fit into your big picture. Evaluate how each one supports your life and your goals.

Balance is a dance between these important components of your life. Allow the music of life to flow through you and embrace this dance!

Seize Your New Day!

Practicing these principles I have outlined and always coming back to an *attitude of gratitude* when "the going gets tough" will undoubtedly give you a solid foundation. Build on this foundation and enjoy your journey as a successful woman entrepreneur!

Amy Nowakowski

Amy Nowakowski is a successful business manager turned author, speaker, and consultant. She has 22 years of technical engineering and program management experience in corporate aerospace. An avid reader and constant student of success principles, Amy is an adjunct professor of business courses at the University of Phoenix. Amy's passion is to provide clients with valuable tools, tips, and techniques to propel their business to achieve higher levels of success utilizing advanced communication skills, solid advice, and even a bit of humor. Tailored training is available. To contact Amy, visit her website: www.InnovativeSolutionsGroup.us, or send an e-mail to amy@InnovativeSolutionsGroup.us. Phone: 877-679-7526.

Chapter Sixteen

Ten Commandments of Successful Goal Setting

Amy Nowakowski

*I*t's been said that when you fail to plan, you plan to fail. That is tough talk, making us each accountable and responsible for our own success or failure. Many do not want to take responsibility for their actions and are happy to put the blame for their failures in life on someone or something else. You truly do have control of your own success and destiny. Women are famous for their expert ability to plan activities, multitask, and carry out detailed plans. They have clear vision to identify what they want and to go after their dreams.

What destiny have you planned? Read on for a method of realizing your most precious goals utilizing the Ten Commandments of Successful Goal Setting.

There are two ways to approach accomplishing goals: planning your work and working your plan, or just being spontaneous. Planning is about results, and not just about creating the plan. The spontaneous approach may *seem* like more fun, but it is really like not having a plan at all. When we spontaneously run our lives by the seat of our pants, we do whatever action seems *right* based on current circumstances and feelings at that moment. The spontaneous approach *may* lead to accomplishing goals, but it is more likely that you will just end up somewhere, anywhere.

Key to accomplishing meaningful long-term success is choosing the right goal to focus on. If your goal is to increase your customer base, you may need to first focus on building sufficient cash flow in other areas of your business. This cash flow will then provide funds to target ideal clients properly so they are the only customers that show up in response to targeted marketing materials.

Spend five minutes to brainstorm all goals that quickly come to mind to identify several potential goals for consideration. Of these goals, some will be more urgent, some will be more important, and some may never need to be done but would just be nice to complete. Steven Covey developed a method of categorizing goals into Urgent vs. Not urgent and Important vs. Not Important categories to clarify which activities to focus on first to provide the best value for the time available. Urgent and important goals will provide the best value, while unimportant and not urgent goals never need to be completed. After utilizing these techniques to identify which goal to focus on, developing a plan to accomplish this newly set goal is the first step toward completion.

A structured approach to goal setting is to plan your work, and then work your plan. The Ten Commandments of Successful Goal Setting will guide you through developing this clear plan for accomplishing goals you have set for yourself or your business. You will also clearly define a goal with a plan of action that when carried out will bring feelings of satisfaction and motivation to set and accomplish more goals. By implementing this process repeatedly, you will become unstoppable.

Commandment One: Be Specific

When a goal is specific, anyone can look at the goal and understand it without asking a multitude of questions. There is also a specific timeframe associated with each goal.

An example of a specific goal is, "I will build my paying client list by 50 new clients by August 1st." This goal has both elements of being specific—it is clear and precise and has an end date. It will be clear to anyone reading this goal when the goal is complete.

Commandment Two: Goals Must be Measurable

In order to know if a goal is accomplished, there must be some way to measure when it is complete. The example goal is measurable because we will know when we have 50 new paying clients by reviewing our database of current clients. We will be able to measure progress along the way and can even break up the goal into smaller more manageable increments. An intermediate goal of adding 5 or 10 clients may be less intimidating than thinking about the longer-term goal of adding 50 clients.

You will know when "you have arrived" at completing your intermediate and end goals when they are measurable.

Commandment Three: Goals Must be Attainable

If we set our goal to "Gain 50 new paying clients by August 1st," and did not have the tools available to get started on the action of reaching the goal, that would not be an attainable goal. If we do not currently have the skills to accomplish the goal and there is no clear plan for gaining that knowledge, we will set ourselves up for failure and discouragement. Whether a new class on identifying and targeting ideal clients is necessary or a new marketing campaign needs development, we know that we will achieve our goal by first acquiring skills and then putting those new skills to work at targeting our ideal clients.

Tools necessary to accomplish intermediate actions must be within reach to get the ball rolling on accomplishing the goal set. Having access to proper tools encompasses being able to afford attending required classes, having access to marketing or design team members to develop new materials that target clients, or other tools to utilize during the action steps of working the goal. Set goals that challenge, but that are within reach.

Commandment Four: Be Realistic

We have all worked on goals at work and in our personal lives that we know are unrealistic. If it is already May and our goal was to "build our paying client list by 50 new clients by June 1st," that seems unrealistic. An unrealistic goal will just serve to discourage the team as they miss mini milestones.

Missing milestones is common with unrealistic goals. Missing milestones without realization that the goal and plan is unrealistic, eventually, will drive the team to give up on the goal completely, and may even cause feelings of personally being a failure. A more realistic goal would be one that we believe can be accomplished in the timeframe we have set, with the skills we have today, or those we will acquire through working the plan. Everything about the goal set must be realistic to stay motivated and always believe in your ability to succeed.

Commandment Five: Write Goals Down

A goal set that is not written down is simply a pipe dream. Pipe dreams will not survive from one week to the next, so we naturally cannot be successful. Not writing a goal down is a setup for failure.

In our example of adding 50 new paying clients, if we do not write our goal down and work our plan, we may actually sabotage ourselves and lose customers. Written goals will drive and motivate your team to plan, complete and celebrate accomplishing goals.

Commandment Six: Visualize Achieving Your Goal

Our subconscious mind is a very powerful tool we can utilize to bring power, peace, and accomplishment into our lives. When we draw our strength from our subconscious mind, we accomplish our goals faster.

To capture the power of your subconscious mind, take time to sit in a quiet place and visualize yourself accomplishing your goal. If you have a team that will work on accomplishing your business goals, you may want to do this as a team exercise. With your eyes closed, visualize how your business will be different when you have completed your goal. What new products or services will you be able to provide to your clients? How will it feel working with your ideal clients who enjoy working with you and are not complainers? Will your profit margin be higher because you can focus on serving the 20% of your clients that add 80% of the revenue? Will you be able to transition your problem clients to your competition, thus freeing you to serve your ideal clients more effectively? Will you enjoy working with your client base more than you do today? Visualize and really feel how you will feel when you have reached your final goal. Take yourself to that place in your mind where you have accomplished your goal and see yourself as you are living your life having successfully completed your goal.

Commandment Seven: Establish Rewards

In order to stay motivated and focused, mini rewards for reaching intermediate milestones are important. Break up your goal into three or four smaller measurable and attainable milestones that you can assign a mini reward.

In our example of adding 50 new clients, you may want to schedule a pizza party or movie day for the team after adding 10 new clients to thank them for their hard work and motivate them to continue working on achieving the end goal. The reward must be personal to the team working the goal, rather than to others, and be appropriate to the goal set. The reward must be something that will motivate you and your team to keep on taking action through to completion. Setting and enjoying these mini rewards will have an incredible impact on your ability to stay focused on accomplishing the end goal.

Commandment Eight: Develop an Action Plan

An action plan details all activities to accomplish coupled with check-up points called milestones. An example of a milestone in our example could be "Thirty new potential clients have been identified," or "Ten new paying clients have been added to our database." The activities are written down, organized into like-task categories, and time-phased in order of what activity to tackle first, second, through to the last task to complete.

Categories of tasks in our example may include "developing marketing materials," "identifying demographics of our ideal client," or "client communication." Specific activities listed in your action plan must be "action statements." This action plan becomes a sort of organized "To Do" list. Completing each activity in the action plan in order will propel you closer to reaching your end goal until you have completely accomplished all milestones and activities and have realized your goal. Your action plan includes specific individual actions you will take that are each individually measurable and specific that you can assign to a team member to work autonomously.

Developing a detailed action plan is one of the most important commandments, and it will be more effective if created as a team exercise.

Commandment Nine: Take Action

A detailed plan is only a plan without life if there is no action. You will not get closer to accomplishing your goal by simply creating your goals, writing them down, and creating an action plan. You must take action to get closer to reaching your goal. As you work on carrying out the action plan, you may find a need to remain flexible and be willing to change the action, timeframe, or method to accomplish the action if the original plan does not work as expected.

Commandment Ten: Record Progress

Once you have created your action plan to accomplish your goal and started taking action, you will stay motivated by recording progress toward activity completion and celebrating with mini rewards. If properly planned, task completion is on time with expected quality. If not, tasks may be harder than expected, take longer than planned, and possibly not have the quality expected. Again, be flexible with the action plan developed, willing to modify the timeframe, budget, or method to assure success in completing goals. Continue recording progress and taking action until each activity and milestone is completed.

Then, remember to celebrate your success! You deserve it!

Anne Berryhill

Anne Berryhill is a lifelong entrepreneur. Currently she is growing her personal training and nutrition business. She has numerous years of business experience under her belt in a variety of industries. Her mission is to help people become their personal best through fitness and nutrition and the realization of their dreams. Always known to have numerous projects in the hopper, she is also CEO of Catch Like a Pro, an online business that focuses on developing catchers for higher levels of baseball. She lives with her high school sweetheart husband, Damon, and their two sons, Josh and Jake, in Southern California. To reach her by phone, call 949-240-4205, or visit her websites:

www.YourFatFighter.com
www.AnneBerryhill.com
www.CatchLikeAPro.com

Chapter Seventeen

You are Stronger Than You Think!

Anne Berryhill

$\mathcal{A}$ s a strength and wellness mentor, I have had the honor of mentoring and training clients to become their personal best. But the road to that personal best is not always easy or clearly marked!

Oftentimes when I have spelled out a strength or wellness plan for someone, their immediate response is, "I can't do that!" Somehow they have never been able to tap into the reservoir of physical and mental strength that is in all of us.

I am reminded that people drastically underestimate their own strength and their strengths. Many people need a mentor to assist them with closing the gap between what is and what is desired. But in the end, it is you who must summon the inner strength to start, run, and finish the race.

Here are some visuals and tools to access the strength that is inside of you!

Run Through the Finish Line!

Let me explain. When you are taking on a challenge, whether it is physical, mental, or emotional, you set your sights on what and how you want things to look like when you get there. That is the "goal' or the "finish line."

When racers are focused on the finish line in sports, their focus is actually beyond the actual line or goal. Therefore, they end up having power, momentum, and a final push to edge out their competition.

What if we looked at our goals in that way? Would we limp, slither, gimp, or stroll to the goal? Or would we use all the momentum and strength it took to get to that line and fly by so that nothing could break our stride?

I encourage people to focus their energies just beyond the goal so that they are in peak form when they cross that goal line!

Physically – Finishing all your weightlifting reps with the same form and power as the first!

Mentally - Seeing yourself receiving the goal and the side benefits with finishing strongly.

Emotionally – Focus on the resolution of conflicts and difficulties and the satisfaction of knowing that you lasted and remained standing.

Self-Coaching

What people forget is that while there are great coaches and mentors all around, our own powers of self-coaching are underused. Many people I know are in a habit of putting themselves down when they talk about themselves or their abilities. Have you ever said something to yourself that if your best friend would have said that to you, you would have been crushed? Since when is it okay to speak to yourself in a way that you would not accept from anyone else on the planet?

The positive alternative to that is to use self-coaching. Self-coaching gets the words flowing through your mind that you need to hear, that you deserve to hear, and want to hear. Try these on for size:

I KNOW I can do that!
This is easy for me!
Every time I do this, I succeed!
I was put on this planet for a reason!
I RUN through the finish line!

I like to use these types of statements to "cover" negative ones that sneak in. What I mean is, say something positive after experiencing negative self-talk. This way, the last words you hear are positive. If all else fails, tell yourself to "knock it off" and leave you alone, like you'd do if another person was badgering you!

Personal Best

Personal best refers to living in a comparison-free environment. We all have a level of performance or achievement that represents the very best we can do with what we have. Luck plays a part, so do genetics and attitude.

Too often, I find people who compare themselves to someone else and become completely blind to the accomplishments and blessings that they already possess.

We obsess about our bodies, grades, bank accounts, test scores, kids, jobs, marriages, and how they measure up to what we perceive outside of our world. Instead, if we embrace what tools and talents we each have and maximize those, our hearts become full and there will no longer be room for comparison or disappointment.

Strive to be the best you that you can be; then you will contribute your unique something to the world. Let go of impossible expectations that you have for yourself and strive to be the best YOU that you can be!

Accept Help

Admittedly, this one has been a tough one for me to embrace. I have the superwoman mentality, and I know that I am not alone. It took someone on the outside sharing that observation with me for me to start to make a change. When you need to do something major in your lives (deliver a baby, paint the house, build a pool), it makes sense to consult an expert.

Oftentimes, there are much smaller challenges that we simply do not allow ourselves the wonderful blessing of outside assistance. Trust me, this does not make you weak or incapable.

On the contrary, if you take someone else's aid, you help them to fulfill their mission for their life. You may be able to juggle multiple tasks or deadlines, but look around; there are people around waiting to help you ease your heavy burden. This can only happen if you allow this to happen. When you do, there will be a dual blessing with no negative side effects. Even if someone performed a task that fell short of your standards, enjoy the fact that someone cared enough for you to help.

We were put here to help each other. But in order to let that happen, someone is the helper and someone is the HELPED. Let that help in when you have it—it will make your day and someone else's, also!

Never Stop Believing

During the different stages of our lives, we may be inclined to listen to naysayers and dream busters. We might actually start to buy into the idea that we don't actually have the goods to get to and deserve our goal. THIS IS DEAD WRONG!

When you have a dream or an idea or a project you can see clearly, never stop believing that it is yours. For a good part of my life, I heard, "That is a great idea, but that will never work." Even when that person was no longer in my life, I still could hear those words at the starting point of every new plan. Finally, I learned that it was that person's own filter of life that directed them to try and save me from failure. Well guess what, it only saved me from success!

Hold on tightly to your goals, dreams, plans, ideas, songs, etc.! They are a gift bestowed on you for a purpose. Never, ever let the fear of another person stop you from fully investing your heart and passion into achieving your plans. If the plans do not pan out or research shows it is not viable, open up because the next idea and dream is coming! Our passions are a gift to us to help and define our purpose for our time here. Never stop believing that what you dream is good to dream because it is YOUR dream.

Arsenia Rendon

Raised in a small Los Angeles suburb, Arsenia Rendon was a stand out at an early age because she understood the value of a good work ethic. Applying this effort, she excelled at academics, the performing arts, and martial arts. Arsenia received her Bachelors of Science degree from USC's Marshall School of Business and shortly thereafter received her Masters in Business Administration. She is currently a successful Real Estate Investor and Business Entrepreneur with a conviction for helping other people achieve their financial dreams. A devoted Christian wife, she is married to her college sweetheart, Ozzy Rendon, and resides in Cerritos, CA. To reach Arsenia, contact her at (310) 227-7675 or send an email to arsenia.rendon@gmail.com. To learn more about Nouveau Riche, the only Real Estate Education Company with ACE Credit Recommendation status, check out these websites:

www.reinvestorsolutions.com/ozinvestments/
www.nruniversity.com
www.investorconcierge.com

Chapter Eighteen

Discovering The New 'YOU'

Arsenia Rendon

*M*y decision to enter in the real estate investing and direct sales business began with the simple desire to create wealth and financial freedom. In your quest for success, you have probably read plenty of books outlining 'Success Factors for Entrepreneurs' or 'Key Elements of a Successful Business.' I am not here to provide you with another To-Do list; rather I am here to help you understand the most important element to success. That component is learning to become the best YOU.

Success is a state of mind; it is a state of being. Many people are looking for the technical know-how to run a business but fail to understand that the business begins and ends with them. What happens in between is your journey to becoming the best YOU. Success in business will never be achieved if you do not have the core belief that you are already successful. This belief is your wellspring of life. When your business is not producing as planned, you must have this conviction to draw from.

Let me ask you this question. If I were to pick up a rock and release it from my grasp, what would happen? It would fall right back to the ground. How did you know this would occur? The reason you knew is because there is a certainty in the outcome. It is engrained in your being to believe that this is fact. If I told you it would float up in the air, you would stand your ground and boldly tell me I was wrong.

Have you ever asked yourself 'Why am I not successful?' or 'Why is everyone else succeeding but me?' In those moments of doubt, you need to center yourself and draw from the conviction that you are a successful woman. This belief has to be engrained in you, and you must believe in yourself. You must hold steadfast to this truth.

As certain as you are about the rock falling to the ground, you must be as certain about yourself and your ability to be successful.

Even though you may not always feel successful, you have to reach deep inside and pull from within. I guarantee there are going to be people who say 'No' to you and to your product. There will be times when sales are not at their highest, times when it seems when everyone else's business is flourishing but yours, and times when the world seems to have cornered you into a wall; but, my friend, it is in these times when you must boldly stand your ground and accept no other belief about yourself.

Once you begin to operate from this premise of self-confidence, you will begin to embrace the challenges of entrepreneurship in a different light. You will no longer be afraid to take the necessary risks needed to produce results. But take note; you will still be faced with obstacles. Regardless of how much a businesswoman believes in herself, she does not always feel like she is succeeding when challenges arise in her business.

There were times in my life when my direct sales business was not thriving. I was consumed with the need to know the exact words and phrases in order to be able to negotiate a deal or get a person to purchase real estate investment education. My belief in myself fluctuated because I started with the premise of 'wanting to be successful'. I failed to realize that all along I was already successful. When the going got tough, I did not have a well to draw from.

My friend, if you are to achieve greatness in any business, it starts with having a core fundamental belief in yourself.

As you begin to accept the fact that you are a successful woman, you will be better equipped to handle what life throws in your direction. You need to know that it is okay to not be perfect. Success does not equal perfection. It never did. So, how is it you handle your areas of improvement without compromising the fact that you are already successful?

To answer this question, I would like to share with you a profound moment in my journey to becoming the best me. One night, my business partner and I decided to have dinner with one of the Nouveau Riche University instructors. We proceeded to ask him to share with us the single quality that has attributed to his many accomplishments. I thought he was going to say, "Building a solid network of buyers and sellers" or "Becoming excellent in one of the real estate investment strategies," but what he said had an unexpected impact in my business.

He said, "In all of the years I have been an entrepreneur and real estate investor, the one thing I attribute to my success is having learned to *forgive myself.*"

The ability to forgive oneself is the greatest gift one can give to themself.

We, as women, have a tendency to be our own worst critic. Our character flaws are unnecessarily magnified within our own eyes. It is not uncommon for us carry the chains of failure forward into our next business ventures. Remember, the goal is not to be perfect. Perfection can never be attained, so how do you throw off these chains and move forward in your business with a clean slate? In your moments of falling short, you need to draw from the strength of your heart and gently, without reserve, gift yourself with forgiveness. Understand your flesh and your heart will fail, but you posses an inner strength that is far greater than your flesh and blood. This strength empowers you to continue along the journey in overcoming your imperfections to becoming the best you.

When your ship sails from your sight, it does not mean the journey ended; it just means the river bends. You must remain centered and resolute to carry on your journey, for it is along this journey of developing yourself and developing your character that your innermost desires come to fruition. To sum it up, business is about constantly working on your character to become the best you can be. It is your character and not your circumstances that make up you. When the river bends, you need to remember you are still the captain of your ship.

Character can only be developed and modified when exposed to hardship. Hardships are key ingredients in making and developing a better you.

Helen Keller perfectly illustrates this point by saying, *"Character cannot be developed in ease and quiet. Only through experiences of trial and suffering can the soul be strengthened, vision cleared, ambition inspired, and success achieved."*

Difficulties in relationships, business ventures, and life in general provide the means and ability for your character to take shape. My aim is for you to sharpen the character you already possess. You have strengths, weaknesses, tendencies, insecurities, thought processes, likes, dislikes, morals, and the list goes on. In order for your character to be refined, it must be exposed to adversity and hardship. It is not the absence of adversity that makes you great, but rather it is the resolve to hold steadfast when you are put to the fire. How can you ever rise to the challenge if there is no challenge? Challenges are what make it conducive for your character to be reestablished, reshaped, and refined.

Now that you understand that adversities are necessary means for your character to transform, how does a person begin to sharpen her character?

Your habits are the birthplace of your character. How were your habits established? Did your habits form randomly, or did you establish them with intent? For example, when the average person gets hungry, she will randomly reach for something to satisfy her appetite. In contrast, when a professional athlete eats, she will eat with intent. She will purposefully consume the best meals that will allow her to achieve peak performance.

Ask yourself this question, "Do I have good habits?" Do you have a habit of starting something and not finishing it? Do you have a habit of looking at everyone else's faults but not taking the time to look at your own? Do you have a habit of arriving late to work or to appointments? Is it your habit to follow a schedule or simply 'wing it'? When falling short, do you possess the habit of forgiving yourself? What are your habits like? Were your habits purposefully developed with the intent to make you great, or were they randomly created?

Over the course of your life, you developed your habits by repeating the same action in the same manner under the same circumstance. Your habits are consistent and occur in the *'uneventful and commonplace hours'* of your life. Your habits are formed and reinforced in your daily activities. It is what you do, what you think, how you act, minute by minute and hour by hour on a consistent basis that determines who you are.

A prosperous business begins by developing better habits. How do you develop better habits? Identify your bad ones and decide to replace them with better ones. The beauty about life is you have choices. If you consistently choose better actions, these actions will form into better habits. The more you choose, the easier the choice becomes, and your good habits begin to dictate your life. You need to watch your actions for they become habits. Watch your habits, for they become character. Watch your character for it becomes your destiny.

My life has been transformed in many tremendous ways. Nouveau Riche University provided me with the vehicle to acquire multiple investment properties in a short amount of time and make more money in one month than I used to make in one year. Nouveau Riche developed the concept of a new 'U' or new University for real estate investors and entrepreneurs, and part of this concept was creating an environment for me to become the best me. The new 'U' was designed for you to become the new 'You'. With the help from faculty and friends and putting these principles into practice, I have been fortunate to experience the financial fruits of my achievements. Nouveau Riche University has nurtured and reinforces core beliefs that guide me through all of my business ventures.

My journey called 'life' is far from being over, but I can stand boldly before you and declare that no matter what life throws my way, I already know, deep in my core, I am successful!

In closing, I want to share with you how Nouveau Riche University (NRU) can assist you in achieving your dreams in becoming the new 'You'. NRU is a brand new concept in higher education and business entrepreneurship. We are the new 'U'niversity of the 21st century, and we provide our students the EPIC solution for wealth creation.

E- Education
We provide world-class real estate investment education tailored to meet YOUR specific needs. We are the only Real Estate Education System that has been awarded The American Council on Education's college credit recommendation status. No other program can stack up against our education.

P- Properties
You can increase your net worth with a simple click of the mouse. We provide our students with property opportunities nationwide that cashflow positively and have equity.

I- Income
Real estate investing provides passive income, but this aspect of NRU provides massive income along with all of the benefits of owning your own business.

C-Community
You will connect with a community of like-minded business entrepreneurs and real estate investors. You will be encouraged, challenged, and motivated to achieve more. They will prompt you and carry you along in your journey to becoming the best 'You'. If you did not believe in yourself before, you will begin to. If you

never learned how to forgive yourself, we will show you how. New habits will be developed, and your character will transform.

If you're looking to change your life, if you're looking for financial freedom, if you are looking to create wealth faster than you ever thought possible, and you are ready to step up, Nouveau Riche University welcomes 'YOU' to the new 'U'.

If you would like more information, feel free to contact me at arsenia.rendon@gmail.com.

April Dangerfield

April Dangerfield has developed three computer-related businesses. An authority in a software program created by NASA and the Army Corps of Engineers, she also developed the SE7 Chip, an Electro-magnetic protection device. April applies her expertise to the field of Biofeedback and Quantum Energy Medicine technology. She interfaces with The L.I.F.E. System, (Living Information Forms Energy). This non-invasive, drug-free program electro-magnetically identifies and measures 7,000 different conditions within the body and calibrates frequencies to assist in achieving optimal health. April's passion is to infuse her technological background to dramatically impact her clients' health. April, along with her husband, resides and practices in Cardiff by the Sea, a quaint beach town just outside San Diego, CA. Contact April at 760-632-7774 or april@SubtleEnergyLLC.com, or visit:

www.SubtleEnergyLLC.com
www.TheEnlightenmentNetwork.com
www.SpecType.com

Chapter Nineteen

To Your Health

April Dangerfield

*H*ave you ever tried to get a pint of dirty, old car oil out of your long blond hair? Twenty years ago, I had to meet that challenge…. all because, as a recently divorced, single mother of two young children, I felt compelled to learn how to be fully responsible for my own life while taking care of my 7 and 10 year olds full time.

My kids and I had such a great time discovering one another and our powerful threesome. We quickly became "The Three Amigos," complete with black shirts and the Steve Martin, Martin Short, and Chevy Chase dance routine.

Along came summer vacation. Enter the necessary baby sitter. From the get-go, I knew we were in trouble. It took all of two weeks before I discovered that my son was rebelling against his sitter by setting fires up on the roof, and my daughter at her ripe old age of eight, with hands planted on her hips, was articulately firing the babysitter on a daily basis. Apparently, the arrangement wasn't serving the purpose I had intended.

It was obviously time to start working from home, where my two little amigos and I could continue to rub shoulders and keep track of each other.

With a little pluck and a lot of luck, I bumbled my way into a one-of-a-kind home-based business that gave me unique access to service Military Contracts. In spite of the fact that my schedule was somewhat erratic when the work came pouring in, my kids and I flourished.

The harder I worked, the clearer I became that retirement and passive income were the worthiest goals I could set for myself. Along the way, I'd been hearing about Robert Allen's "No Money Down" seminars and decided to investigate. By the end of a week-long workshop—I got the message. Boy, did I. Within a month, I was the proud owner of an eight-unit apartment building in the Normal Heights neighborhood of San Diego.

The following week found the kids and me in a brilliantly conceived self-esteem workshop that my now 28 and 32 year old children remember fondly to this day.

And about that apartment house.... The kids and I painted it, caulked it, patched it, replaced bathroom fixtures, kitchen fixtures, garbage disposals, cabinet hardware, mended curtains, replaced water heaters, bug bombed, hauled trash and arranged for replacement carpet on a regular basis. Phew!

Challenging myself to move to the next level of personal growth, I enrolled in the Forum in September, 1993. At the introduction workshop, I turned to the man seated to my left and met Michael, my husband to be. Three months later, we were married. A wonderful 13 years later, I am still married to one of the most happy, spiritually balanced, and accepting persons I have ever known. It was Michael who truly introduced me to the whole process of mentoring. He mentored me in moving deeply into my own essence of spirit, with a deeper understanding and purpose to move forward in ways I never thought possible. He believed in me then more than I believed in myself.

About four years ago, I became seriously interested in alternative health. I wanted to help others. This was a need I felt deeply. It was easy to visualize really helping others. I could feel the tremendous satisfaction and gratification of giving service to others.

The healing modalities that immediately began to present themselves to me were powerful and broad based. I was able to learn the application of these alternative healing agents with amazing ease. I shared the results I was personally receiving with my friends, and before I knew it, clients were showing up at my door. The primary complementary modalities I worked with are these six:

Young Living Essential Oils

The SE7 Chip for Neutralizing Electromagnetic and Geopathic Stress   (Designed and Developed by a Naturopathic Doctor and myself)

Emotional Freedom Technique

Scenar (A handheld healing device created for the Russian Cosmonauts orbiting in space)

Holistic Enterprises

Amazon Herb Company

Two years ago, I was introduced to the ultimate alternative healing technology. Without question, The LIFE System is state-of-the-art.

In December 2006, Dr. Thorton Streeter, DSc, CEO and Founder of Centre for Biofield Sciences, flew at his own expense to the 2nd Annual Quantum Life Symposium in Puerto Vallarta, Mexico, to give his testimonial that of the 190 medical and alternative devices his center has evaluated, The LIFE System was #1.

The L.I.F.E. System is a computer software biofeedback program which identifies energetic imbalances in the body (every human health problem, regardless of its description, is an energetic imbalance in the body). Your body is energy. All thoughts are energy. All energy can be identified by frequencies. All frequencies are able to be identified. When you introduce positive energy into your body, you create a positive energetic life. Past thoughts, actions and environments imprint specific energy into your body.

Energetic imbalances can be identified through The LIFE System software and hardware. The good news is that any thought, action, or environmental toxin can be balanced or neutralized by feeding back the appropriate electro-magnetic signals that produce positive energy in the body.

Richard Gerber, MD, author of *Vibrational Medicine* (the definitive survey of energetic and alternative healing methods), states that "Recent studies in the area of biofeedback techniques show that directed mind cannot only control various autonomic body functions such as skin temperature and pain, but can also repair the body."

Ryan and Karen Williams of Quantum Life, LLC have been my mentors in learning, working with and teaching how to use The LIFE System. Working with the system on myself over the last 2 years, I have lost 10 years in appearance. In April 2007, my mother-in-law asked me, "What kind of makeup are you using? …You look great!" My honest reply was, "I don't use makeup." I feel fantastic, and I am clearer and happier than I have ever been in my life.

From the results that my clients, my husband, and I have received, I can categorically state that everyone should own this technology or have access to a health care provider with this system.

My greatest pleasure, in addition to facilitating client sessions on The LIFE System, is mentoring and teaching others to use the cutting edge technology themselves. Under the tutelage of Ryan and Karen Williams, I have learned the ins and outs of the system so thoroughly that I have been offering "Webinars" (seminars held live over the internet using video cameras that are attached to each person's computer) since 2006. My students have challenged me to explore and find answers to every possible question related to biofeedback energy medicine. In turn, I have discovered the simplest, clearest ways to instruct them in how to use and derive the maximum benefit from the technology for their own and their clients' healing.

In closing, I want to share with you the principles and values that have guided me through these last 21 amazing years, in which my life has unfolded and evolved in the most magical ways.

First, learn to trust your inner voice. Let yourself embrace your own best instincts and follow your heart–no matter how unfathomable the direction may seem at the moment.

Second, if you don't like a thought that keeps popping up inside of you, know that you absolutely have the power to shift your thinking. Just ask yourself this: "What do I want right now instead of this thought?"

I recommend that you use positive affirmations of what you do want. You practice positive thinking and you visualize yourself at every opportunity, living the life you want to be living. And please be open to letting the computer age help you in receiving the life you deserve. As your negative physical, emotional, and mental energy clears away, you will open to a lighter, brighter, happier LIFE.

Patricia Fripp

Patricia Fripp, CSP, CPAE is a San Francisco-based executive speech coach, sales trainer, and award-winning professional speaker on Change, Customer Service, Promoting Business, and Communication Skills. She is the author of *Get What You Want!*, *Make It, So You Don't Have to Fake It!*, and Past-President of the National Speakers Association. She can be reached at: PFripp@Fripp.com, by telephone at 1-800 634-3035, or visit her website: http://www.fripp.com.

Chapter Twenty

Have you Built a Business?
Or Just a Job?

Patricia Fripp, CSP, CPAE

$\mathcal{M}$y friend, Michael Sipe, brought home to me the tremendous difference between building a business versus a job working for yourself. Mike is a mergers and acquisitions specialist, arranging and negotiating the sale of (you guessed it) businesses. One of his clients was Bob.

Bob had been very successful for 30 years in corporate America, but he had dreamed of having his own business. When he turned 50, he took early retirement, cashed in his retirement accounts and put all his money into starting his own business. His wife, Mary, kept the books and ran the office. Bob was very customer-service oriented, a big, athletic, can-do kind of guy with huge energy. Everyday, he was right in the middle of everything, working with clients, staff, and vendors, and having a grand time. He was profiled by a major business journal as an example of a successful entrepreneur. Bob and Mary planned to work the business for 10 years and then sell it for $1.5 million, retire to Seattle to play with their grandchildren and live happily ever after. They were living the American dream. Everything was perfect.

Except that one day Bob woke up and noticed he wasn't feeling well. The doctor told him that if he didn't get out of the business, he'd be dead in six months: "Sell the business, reduce your stress level, and chances are you'll live a few more years."

Bob and Mary were referred by their CPA to Michael Sipe for professional advice. Mary was in a panic. Bob, as you can imagine, was devastated. Bob broke down. Mary broke down. Mike, who had never met them before, ended up in tears, too. Bob said, "Mike,

I don't want to sell my business. I LOVE my business. But, I don't have any choice. Can you help me?"

Mike asked what they planned to do. Bob told him their retirement plan called for $1.5 million, so they needed Mike to sell the business for that amount. Mike examined the business thoroughly and discovered it wasn't worth that amount--and given how it was being operated, likely never would be. The problem, Mike told them, was that Bob hadn't really built a "business." He had really just created a "job", working for himself. He had kept himself right in the middle of things, needing to approve every decision, know every customer, and do everything connected with the business. He'd even named it after himself. He had a dozen employees, so it LOOKED as if he had a business, but, in fact, Bob WAS the business. When Bob couldn't work effectively anymore, the business didn't seem to work well, either. Revenues and profits started dropping off. Bob hadn't built a business with any particular value beyond his own participation. Until Mike pointed this out, Bob hadn't realized it, and no one else had, either.

Mike said, "Bob, I don't know how to break this to you at such a bad time, but you'll be lucky to get $300,000 for the business." Bob and Mary had no significant outside money, no safety net for their retirement. Reluctantly, Bob told Mike, "I don't want to die from stress, and I certainly hope we can do better than $300,000. Please do the best you can for us."

Fortunately, Mike was able to get four prospective buyers involved in competitive bidding. He sold the company for $400,000. It was a bittersweet victory. Mike helped Bob leave the business with dignity and transfer it to a new owner who is doing well. Although the company sold for more than expected, it was a far different price than Bob and Mary had dreamed of, particularly after taxes.

The good news is that Bob is alive. Bob and Mary ARE spending a lot of time playing with their grandchildren. The bad news is, its because they've had to move in with their children as they can't afford to live in their own house. And Mary works at a low-paying job, not for pleasure or stimulation, but because they need the money.

"None of this had to happen," says Mike. "If only someone had grabbed hold of Bob and told him, 'You're not building anything of value here. You only have a job, not a business."

"This happens more often than you'd think," Mike explains. "And when it does, the business is rarely worth what the owner thinks it is. If you stopped showing up, how well would your business do? Would it still be going a year from now? In five years?"

A very different situation is typified by Tom, a wiry outdoorsman and martial artist. He started his own business, about the same time Bob did. Five years later, Tom was talking with his martial arts "sensei" (which means "master"). His sensei told him, "Tom, your rice bowl is full."

"What do you mean?" Tom asked.

"You have a good net worth. Your kids are out of college, you've got a house in Saratoga and another house in Palm Springs, you travel around the world, you're in great health, and you've got a good business. You've also got things you still want to experience. How much is 'enough'? Your rice bowl is full. Why don't you sell your business and go do some of the things you still want to do?"

Tom was referred to Michael Sipe by his banker for advice. "Mike," he said, "my rice bowl is full."

"That's really nice," said Mike. "So how can I help you?"

Tom explained and said he'd decided to sell his business and would be happy to get $1 million. Mike evaluated the operation and found a completely different situation from Bob's. Tom wasn't managing the business. He was its leader and strategic director. A group of highly motivated and superbly skilled managers and employees ran the company. The facilities were immaculate; the equipment was in great shape. There was a strong balance sheet and no debt. The organization had been consistently profitable. The company wasn't large, but it was beautifully designed. Forty-five days later, Mike closed the sale of the business for $1.5 million--in cash. Tom is now off pursuing all his other interests. His rice bowl is full.

Mike's advice to anyone thinking of buying a business is this. If you want your own company, set it up so that you can sell it whenever you want to (or have to). Build your organization so that it has real value beyond your participation. There are four simple rules for doing this.

1. Put yourself in charge of working ON your business, not IN it. Build your business so it can run without you on a day-to-day basis. Break your responsibilities into different functions that other people could perform. Don't be the only one who can handle certain tasks. Cross-train your employees so that each can handle several different duties when necessary. Hire people with management potential. Then develop them.

2. Make sure your business looks good. Appearance DOES matter. A clean, well maintained, attractive company is much easier to sell, and commands a higher price than a tired, dirty, run-down operation.

3. Get an outside opinion on your company's value on a regular basis. You get periodic physical exams to assure your body is healthy; doesn't it make sense to have a professional checkup on the health, liquidity and value of your company?

4. Build a profitable company. This point may seem obvious, but many entrepreneurs come to Mike with the belief that simple longevity matters, saying, "We've been in business for 10 years, so our company must be worth $10 million." Or they think that sales volume determines price. "Our sales are $3,000,000, so we want two times sales for the company." When Mike asks about their profits, they reply, "Well, we hope to make a profit SOMEDAY..."

Mike's advice is, "Set financial goals and meet them. If your business isn't making significant amounts of money right now, it's highly unlikely you will be able to walk away with anything to show for your hard work."

Finally, have an exit strategy for how you plan to leave your business. Don't just assume everything will work out. Seek professional help and develop a viable plan with contingencies. Everyone leaves their business sometime, but as Bob discovered, we don't always know when.

We offer this article on a nonexclusive basis. You may reprint or repost this material as long as Patricia Fripp's name and contact information is included. PFripp@Fripp.com, 1-800 634-3035, http://www.fripp.com

Gail Freeman

Gail D. Freeman is living her passion as a RN and singer. This on the rise speaker and writer resides in El Monte, California. Gail is currently an MBA candidate at the University of Phoenix. She loves to inspire people to live their passion and life to the fullest. Gail can be contacted at Gailpraizes2@aol.com.

Chapter Twenty-One

Living Your Passion

Gail Freeman

"*O*h Gail, don't you know you're the only one who is actually doing in your life what you want. The rest of us do what is takes to just get by." I'll never forget hearing those words as I looked at my friends. My mind whirling, I wondered in amazement why anyone would ever do anything that they really didn't want to do. I asked, "Why would you do that?" My friends' responses left me wondering how many people in this world just live to exist, giving up rather than fighting for what they want, choosing to live in the mundane rather than live their passion.

Of course, I had an answer for each one of them. Just stop doing what is mundane and begin to live your passion. Do what you want; do what brings you joy. Do not settle just to get by or make a living. Money, while it brings pleasure, will not bring happiness or joy if you do not like what you do or how you live life. If you know what you want in life and it involves going back to school or changing professions, do what it takes, take a chance. You have nothing to lose but the fear that is holding you captive.

Another lesson I learned that day is most of us would rather live in what we know even if we are miserable rather than risk being happy or risk failing. Fear is a prison and will keep you from your passions, dreams, goals, and visions. Go forward in life, take the risk, write out and, stick to an action plan, and live your passion. Living your passion has challenges, especially the challenge of change. Change means getting out of the status quo, taking a risk and growing. I have heard that the only person who likes change is a baby: he or she wants their diapers changed. In each of us is exists a passion, a dream, and it wants to be born and be set free.

In the early 1960's, the show "The Nurses" hit the airwaves. The show was a medical drama about the life and times of a nurse.

Shirl Conway played the Head Nurse and Zina Bethune played a student nurse {her name on the show was Gail]. Every week, my Mom and I watched the show. I remember thinking that would be really amazing to be a nurse. I could save lives. The passion was awakened in my soul; I made a decision that would impact me for the rest of my life. "I am going to be a nurse. I will be one of women in white helping to save lives, treating the injured and comforting the dying." The passion became my dream, the dream my vision, and my vision my reality as I entered nursing school at seventeen and a half.

During my entire school life, every course I took was geared at becoming a nurse. I told my parents "I am going to be a nurse when I grow up." They looked at me and smiled, you know, the look that says you're just a kid; you will change your mind as you get older. Yet, I was singled-minded. Each time an adult asked what I wanted to be when I grew up, my response was the same; I am going to be a nurse. So, when I was ten, my mom told me, "Gail, you can be whatever you want to be. All you need is the education. If you are going to be a nurse, what classes do you need?" I began to research what was needed. I asked one of my teachers how to go about getting the knowledge I needed to be a nurse. Mr. Falzone, my sixth grade teacher, told me to look it up in the library. So, I did. I needed a college education. Consequently, beginning in the seventh grade, I started college prep courses.

Every time I ran into a discouragement, studying got hard, or friends or relatives told me I couldn't do it, I heard my Mom's voice reminding me that I could be whatever I wanted. All I have to do is study, get the education, and I will be unstoppable. At fourteen and half, I became a Jr. Volunteer. My Mom thought it was a good idea; while supportive of my decision, she wanted to be sure I really wanted to be a nurse. She thought this would help me make the final decision. It was the best time. The staff knew four of us wanted to be nurses; they let us observe procedures normally not approved for volunteers and we did things student nurses did. I loved it. Working in the hospital just solidified my goal, my passion. My mom was right. With determination, a vision, and a plan, I graduated high school, even won a J&J nursing scholarship, and I was accepted by a college and two nursing schools. I was going to live my passion.

Then I hit the wall; no one ever told me that my color would or could stop me. I will never forget the day the director of the nursing school told all of the young women of color we had been accepted because of "Affirmative Action." So, do you think I let that influence me? No way. My mom told me I was unstoppable; I knew I was unstoppable. I proved the director wrong, made the honor roll and, yes, I passed and became a RN. (Oh, did I forget to tell you, part of being passionate is the fighter awakens in you; determination makes you unbeatable.)

Passion is a powerful emotion, an ardent love or boundless enthusiasm. It is excitement, zeal for life, and a delight. Passion is the one feature in your life that no matter what circumstance comes your way, you feel invincible. Is it easy to live your passion? Well yes and no; to live your passion takes work. My advice is to write out your passion, your dream. Keep it in front of you; talk about it with parents, your friends, teachers, and a mentor. Research what it will take to obtain your dream, invest the time in yourself, get an education, and save the money needed to get hold of your passion or get a scholarship. Do what it takes to get what you want.

Whatever they are, your passions can all live. And, yes, you can have more than one—I do. You can actively pursue the goals set before you in life and share the joy with others. I have never regretted my decision to follow my heart, and I still have the greatest joy working as a nurse. Now, I want to share the joy. I have the privilege of speaking to young adults. My advice to them is to develop and live their dreams. You will have to work for the dream/passion, yet the reward of living your passion and doing what you love is worth it. Each of us can accomplish whatever we put our minds, souls, and spirit to gain. Do not settle for the mundane, the everyday, live your life in joy. Find out what your purpose is and go for your passion, live your passion, enjoy your passion, and enjoy life, I do.

Shauna Decker

Shauna Decker is a Fine Artist specializing in Custom Decorative Wall Treatments in San Diego. Her company, Shauna Decker, BFA, is known for its high quality of work, unique creations, and sophisticated European Plasters. She studied at the finest Decorative and Mural Schools in the country. In the summer of 2007, she painted in Rome under the guidance of four of the worlds foremost Decorative Painters in Portraiture, Landscape, Trompe L'oeil, Fresco Murals and Ornamentation. Shauna's continued studies demonstrate her motivation to bring the most innovative, sophisticated Finishes to her clients. Shauna is a licensed contractor in the state of California and does both commercial and residential projects for builders, general contractors, architects, designers and homeowners. Shauna's passion is building businesses and relationships that ensure the highest level of integrity and expertise. Contact Shauna at shauna@shaunadecker.com or phone 760-720-7450. Visit her website at:

www.shaunadecker.com

Chapter Twenty-Two

Follow Your Heart Song

Shauna L. Decker, BFA

Trust yourself, be your authentic self, live your passion…
You are the leader of your destiny…

I am alone in Rome, Italy, writing this from a quaint café; and the truth is that I wouldn't want to be anywhere else…I am about to study under four Master Painters for three weeks. I am a risk taker, and I believe in what I do; and what I do is create outstanding custom decorative wall treatments.

I was not always this way; I had to learn to trust myself and believe in me. It's been a long journey and one I would like to share.

I believe in magic and feel that I create magic every day in my thoughts and actions. My business is Shauna Decker, BFA. "Making magic happen, one detail at a time." I am a fine artist who specializes in custom decorative wall treatments. I only feel good when I am the best at whatever I do!

I was raised in Michigan with an ethical standard of 'do it right the first time or don't do it at all.' When I decided to offer my talents to the commercial and residential clientele, I had to ensure that I provided the highest quality workmanship and artisanship to the consumer and surround that with the highest standards of integrity, which to me means punctuality, day to day accountability, reliable contracts, and impeccable workmanship.

Once I decided to be a Decorative Artist, I sought out the finest Decorative Finishing and Faux Finishing Academies in the country to become proficient in exotic, high-end wall treatments and the new skill sets required to produce anything that my eye could see and my imagination could create.

That's why I am here in Rome studying with four of the world's most recognized Decorative Painters. For three weeks, I will be challenged and pushed to go beyond any self-imposed boundaries and unforeseen insecurities. I will come home with four amazing canvases and a lifetime's worth of knowledge. To be in the presence of Masters, in studio, in the birthplace of art, confirms that I am living my passion, and that is my life and my life's work.

I believe as a woman it's a requirement to not second guess our choices, but rather blindly trust ourselves to succeed and persevere until we find our inner sanctuary and our inner power to manifest our dreams.

I was under the impression as a child that I was not a good artist and that an art career is only a hobby. But something in my bones told me that I should go in that direction, and I changed my business major to Fine Art in my last semester. I never looked back. This was the first of many decisions that have enabled me to be successful today.

I wanted to be the BEST in talent and knowledge so I learned from the best people in the field that are known internationally for their work. If you want to be the best, learn from the best. Mentorship has been the cornerstone of success.

My Bachelor of Fine Arts is in Painting. My instructors would criticize my body of work because it was not stylized. I would paint differently with different styles and different subject matter. I was exploring and would get frustrated with the notion that I had to pick one style that was a reflection of myself!

Now as a decorative Artist, I see that as the beginning of my path to be able to paint in any style, any era, and to have the ability to improvise with any materials and tools and magically produce something amazing!

As a little girl, I was surrounded by the daily efforts of two parents striving to build two separate businesses. Entrepreneurism is all I have known most of my life. I have had two fine parents exemplifying what it takes and the wherewithal required to succeed. This was one of the reasons that I got my Contractor's license. I wanted my Decorative Painting business to be legitimate and legal.

One of the most important things I learned in our household was that when money is tight and income is inconsistent, things can and will turn around with concerted focused efforts. YOU make the difference. Believe in yourself and trust yourself to know that you are making the choices and changes that will provide the next opportunity of income for your company. And always, always be willing to do the grunt work when you cannot afford to pay for the labor if it means you can keep the doors open one more day.

The second most valuable lesson I learned is to be your authentic self.

My Business Journey began in 1989 when I was 21. I moved from the comfort of my home to the state of Colorado to start a business with my brother and my mother. ImageSystems, Inc., provided state of the art film and paper from digital files. We were the missing link from digital file to traditional printing presses. It was very cutting edge technology at the time. I was hungry to learn everything all at once.

While being groomed by our banker and our CPA, I was simultaneously attending the University of Colorado in Boulder with an Entrepreneur Curriculum. Additionally, I was enrolled in the National Entrepreneurship Academy (Denver chapter). That was a phenomenal experience for a young entrepreneur. It was the best mentorship program, and it had quite an impact on how to grow a business and understand proper business management and potential pitfalls. The demands were high and the results priceless.

However, when my body told me that I was on the wrong career path, I sold my shares and changed my degree program to Fine Art...and the future began to unfold. I followed my heart. I was not a child prodigy, but I brought all that business acumen I had acquired. One of the things I did immediately was to start a Real Estate Investment Business with my dad, which we had for ten years while I built my Art Career. Today, I still love to invest in real estate and find it a second personal passion.

Overall, on a last note, it's extremely important to find balance in your life. Be wildly successful and still force yourself to make time for yourself and your loved ones.

Shauna L. Decker, BFA

Debbra Sweet

Entrepreneur, Author, Musician, Speaker, Consultant, Coach, Trainer are titles that apply to Sweet Marketing Solutions founder, Debbra Sweet. Exposure to business at an early age and artistic talent in music and writing is the background that Debbra brings to her clients. This unique blend of understanding business systems, value in client relationships, and endless creativity are key elements that Sweet uses to lead her team of professionals to achieving client results in marketing. Never one to 'wait for things to happen,' Debbra opens new doors for her clients and her company in the areas marketing, advertising, and promotions. Her professional experience on stage as a musician and speaker helps her deliver messages in a fresh, motivating way. Always focusing on the end results, Debbra helps to streamline the vastness of marketing so her clients can be comfortably involved when they are working towards achieving marketing growth goals. Contact Debbra at: www.sweetmarketingsolutions.com.

Chapter Twenty-Three

The 4 P's for Success

Debbra Sweet

*P*atience, Persistence, a Positive Attitude, and Passion. Over the years, these words have become my personal mantra. They are cornerstones in the foundation of my success. They resonate with the entrepreneurial spirit and can be a driving force for your success, too. When you endeavor to follow your dreams and become successful–whether it's running your household, being the CEO of a business or becoming the next Mother Teresa--these key factors, when applied, will help your vision come to life.

Undoubtedly, there are times when your desire for something is so strong, the longing intense, and your focus is solely on getting what you want. These emotions can be a motivating force for the entrepreneurial spirit– but it's only the beginning. How do you manifest these feelings into something concrete, visible and real to yourself and those around you? There is a way... and it begins with an understanding that dreams manifested can have the appearance of overnight success, but there's usually a plan behind the success. What's yours? What emotions and actions drive your plan?

It's been said that we live in an 'instant gratification' society. When you're on your way to creating a life that's fulfilling, stable, balanced, happy and rewarding, moments of instant gratification can be 'wins' along the way to achieving your big dreams. However, when you get down to the emotions that create your dreams, you need to walk a different way. You need to create a life that's intentional if your dreams are ever going to become reality. The road to your success will come. Here are a few keys to enjoying the journey along the way.

<u>Patience</u>

Understanding that patience is a key element to success is vital while on your own journey to greatness. The dictionary defines patience as: the bearing of provocation, annoyance, misfortune, or pain, without complaint, loss of temper, irritation, or the like. It's also: quiet, steady perseverance; even-tempered care; and diligence.

Whatever your goals are, if you're going to achieve greatness, you must have patience. There are people who seem to appear 'on the scene' and become an overnight success. In most cases, if you dig deep into their experiences, you'll find that there's been a lot of groundwork, trial and error, and challenges that happened long before they rose to the top. The same is true for you. Your rise to success and greatness doesn't have to take years—but it does take commitment *to want* to make your desires come to life and have the patience to make it happen.

You can't raise a building without having a really strong foundation. Success comes the same way—it takes the laying of a foundation. Your foundation needs to be strong enough to support your dreams. To build it, you need a plan. When planning it, remember that time needs to be your friend—and all your experiences up to this point tie into your dreams. It's easy to become frustrated and impatient when the struggle for your dreams to come to pass seems to take longer than you want. This impatience or anxiety is counter productive.

Patience is a virtue, which means: moral excellence; goodness; righteousness; a good or admirable quality or property, effective force; power or potency. Those last two words, power and potency, speak volumes when understanding how patience ties into your entrepreneurial success. When you have a great platform of patience, you have inherent power and potency to make your dreams manifest.

If you're a believer in the law of attraction or if your guidance comes from a spiritual direction, mastering your emotions so you can consistently walk with patience will get you through many situations and allow you to recognize when opportunities are presenting themselves.

Persistence

It's been documented that many of the best ideas come after many attempts and much failure. Persistence is very important to your success strategy because it tends to become one of the keys in motivation. You need to be motivated to be persistent—yet persistence can drive your motivation, desire and vision to reach what you're striving for.

Persistence also goes hand in hand with patience. In my quests for success, I've endured much rejection. When I knew that what I was pursuing was right, my persistence is one thing that kept me going. One of my earliest experiences of rejection and the impact patience and persistence had on my results was in the area of my music. Performing music professionally has been, and still is, one of my deepest life goals. Early on in my career, I started singing and playing instruments simultaneously. A few years into performing with both areas, I was told flat out (by a teacher, an influence in my life that I admired) that "I wasn't good enough to continue singing – so I shouldn't even bother" to pursue it. Those words hurt me-and I listened—so for the next four years, I didn't sing publicly. I devoted all my public performances to instrumental music, but deep down inside I knew I could also sing and was good at it. Privately, I was persistent in my belief and sang all the time. My belief in my abilities was there, and I persisted to practice.

Four years later, I was performing with a group of musicians who were predominately very talented vocalists. I was a bit shy about singing with them (as those early words still rang in my head), but I was needed to sing for one of the songs. When those other musicians heard me sing, they were shocked. They knew me to be the best instrumentalist in the area, but they didn't know I could sing, as well. All of them genuinely supported me to sing more often and not hide my abilities. I've sung from that day and received recognition, scholarships, professional income, and many awards and medals from both singing and instrumental music.

Many people who appear to 'suddenly make it big' actually have been persistent for 10 years or more. They'll find wins along the way, but often have many attempts with non-success behind the scenes. It's in these moments that you really have a chance to prove yourself, and you need patience and persistence to make the next step. If you're working toward a goal and making measurable, noticeable strides, it's the moments of non-perfection that are the most valuable. By walking with persistence, you can objectively look at what works right along with identifying weak areas. Persistence gives you the 'legs' to make changes in your plans—to refocus, recalculate and then try again. Patience and persistence are closely intertwined to helping you reach the goals and dreams you've always wanted.

Positive Attitude

A third key success factor to helping you be your best and achieve the life you've always wanted is maintaining a positive attitude. Whether you are an optimist, pessimist, or realist, being able to look upon things objectively and view situations completely allows you to see opportunities you might not have noticed before. By identifying opportunities, you can continue with a positive attitude.

It takes a lot of inner courage to walk with a positive attitude, especially during those times when all you see or hear is rejection and negative feedback from others. If you're being patient and have persistence, yet you are not fully receiving the support you genuinely deserve from the outside world, your ability to maintain a positive attitude on the inside will bring to you the opportunities that will make you successful.

For those who are naturally optimistic, this may not be such a stretch. The challenge most optimists face is to ground themselves enough to really get the results they want. As a self-proclaimed 'eternal optimist,' I taught myself to walk with extreme positive thought. Yet, I understand that it is important to have a plan, to be patient and persistent in order to see my optimistic thoughts through to fruition.

If your world is that of a 'realist'—you see things for 'what they really are'—having a positive attitude can be a bit more challenging. It's not impossible. You just need to recognize that your thought process can (and does) have a direct impact on your desired results.

Some people are genuine pessimists. (Others who claim to be are really just overly frustrated with the challenges in their life.) If you really are a pessimist, then having a positive attitude toward an outcome is something that you'll need to practice daily until the results you want start to manifest.

Recently, the focus abounding about the universal law of attraction reveals much about the frequency and vibrations emitted by the real energy of our thought processes. A positive attitude emits positive energy and attracts positive results in life. The opposite also is true. Which do you want?

A positive attitude really needs to be an inside job that is firmly cemented in your belief system. The more successful you become, the more well balanced your life is; the happier you are, the more peaceful and financially well off you are. But, beware that other people who have a negative mindset might try to bring you down.

Overcoming your own fear and self doubt is one thing. Once you have a strong positive belief of your own abilities, you need to look at the people who are part of your everyday life. The influence others can have upon you (whether it's subtle or obvious) has a direct impact on the circumstances in your life. This could be good or bad. Your vision is success--what's the vision of those around you? Take a good look at your circle of influence. If the people you surround yourself with always speak negatively about your dreams and goals, then it's time to change your circle of influence. Positive support on the outside makes it easier to keep your positive attitude strong.

Look at yourself and think about one of your biggest successes. What did you do right? How did you feel along the way? What were you thinking the moment the reality of the success happened? Chances are you felt great. Your mind was strong. You were on top of the world. It is available to think and feel like that every day. It may take practice, but it starts with your simple conscious decision to make it happen.

If others around you start to become negative, condescending, or doubtful of your abilities, then you need to make a choice. You can either: 1) Stay there and listen, maybe take it in and let it start to affect your thinking, or 2) You can stay strong, be positive in your own beliefs and walk away.

Stand right and stand true in your own convictions of what you believe in. Take ownership of your positive beliefs. When you do, there will be people who enter your life who will support you. They will reinforce your positive attitude, and soon you really will be living the life you've only dreamt of.

Passion

The last and most important key success factor in becoming the entrepreneur you've always envisioned is passion. Without passion, your dreams will be only wishes.

There's an old cliché in the business world. It says: "Fake it till you make it." These words can get you going—especially when you're first starting out. Until you actually have some passion to drive your actions, you may end up *always* faking it instead of actually *making it*. Passion is one of the biggest catalysts behind great ideas and true success. It's a strong or extravagant enthusiasm or desire for something. Passion drives the entrepreneurial spirit and will bring your dreams to life. The final cornerstone in the key elements to what it takes to be a successful entrepreneur resoundingly resides in passion. You need patience; you'll have to be persistent. You can learn to view things from a positive perspective; but until you infuse these all with passion, your successes will be limited.

Endeavor to bring the 4 P's into your life. Let them be the four cornerstones of your success. Practice each one daily for a week, then move onto the next, and soon, you will see your dreams become reality.

Robin Jay

Robin Jay is a professional keynote speaker, corporate trainer, and author of the award-winning book, "The Art of the Business Lunch ~ Building Relationships Between 12 and 2" (Career Press, 2006). She is a business expert who speaks on business relationships, networking, sales, customer service, and essential wellness. She is also the president and founder of the Las Vegas Convention Speakers' Bureau (please visit their website at www.LVCSB.com). You are invited to visit her website at www.RobinJay.com, e-mail her at Robin@RobinJay.com, or contact her by calling 702-460-1420.

Chapter Twenty-Four

The Worst Thing That Can Happen to You

Robin Jay

*S*o many of us dream of becoming an entrepreneur—self-employed, successful, able to enjoy financial freedom and live our lives however we choose. You may have thought about how fabulous it would be to wake up at noon, travel when you want, or even work until the wee hours of the morning when necessary.

Many of us grow tired of working for someone else and doing everything their way. We believe we have a better method, a more clever idea, or we just want to be on our own to spread our wings and fly. In spite of these ideals, most of us are still reluctant to take the leap of faith necessary to become an entrepreneur.

Those who have succeeded encourage others enthusiastically, from sharing how they gave away their stuffy business suits and dresses to how much they love their new lives and their freedom. Most of them are also eager to share the downside, wearing it like a badge of courage. They detail their day-to-day existence…how they work from the time they get up until late at night and how days off are a thing of the past. And while it may be true that "when you do what you love for a living, you never work another day in your life," your friends may not be as quick to tell you that you may also never again have a "real" day off, free of responsibility or care! Owning your own company or running your own business can have some drawbacks, but the joy of pursuing your passion outweighs even the worst of those.

The Leap

You feel passionately about pursuing your dream. Your financing is in order. You have a business plan. Yet you are still reluctant to move forward.

163

When it comes to walking away from the familiar to pursue the unknown, there is a lot to consider. Women can be very nurturing, loving parents, stay-at-home moms or "superhero" multi-taskers...working outside the house and coming home each day to the "second shift" of caring for their family. Women have others who depend on them, which adds to the risk of any new venture.

Our creative imaginations may vividly conjure up all the ways in which we may fail. We are certainly never at a loss when we focus on what could go wrong. What if we run out of money? What if we aren't able to do what's necessary to succeed? What if we are unprepared for unexpected crises? What if we are making a HUGE mistake? If we succeed OR fail, what will happen to those around us?

This is where a mentor can help. Get help as you begin, rather than waiting until it's too late. Choose someone who has successfully done what you want to do and who can help you achieve your dreams. Mentors love to help – and can save you costly steps along the way. Find the right one for you and work with her. She will be worth her weight in gold in her encouragement, experience, and enthusiasm for you and your dream.

As a business relationship expert, I always suggest you stack the deck in your favor...and there is no better way to do that than by taking advantage of someone else's experience.

The Worst Thing That Can Happen to You

Ask yourself, *"What is the worst thing that can happen to me if EVERYTHING goes wrong? What is the worst case scenario?"* Be honest with yourself and let your imagination run wild. Are you able to come up with a situation in which you feel certain you would NOT be able to recover? I bet not!

We tend to get bogged down in the land of "What If." What if I fail? What if I look foolish? What if I lose everything and have to go back to my old job? Well....what IF? I can't begin to tell you how many times asking myself this question has helped me to move forward...because I know that whatever horror I can imagine, nothing in reality will even come close. There is nothing that can happen professionally that I won't be able to work through or even benefit from. Here's an even better question: What if you never try and don't know what you're missing?

Successful people assert, "If you always do what you've always done, you'll always get what you've always gotten." Unless you are willing to try something new, you will never know the rewards that can come from such action. If you stay in your comfort zone, you may have some laughs or rewards along the way, but you are ultimately just playing the same old tape over again and again. When you set out to live your dream, success is guaranteed.

Ask yourself, "What if I move toward my dream and fail?" Failure is never 100%. Sometimes failure in one field simply leads us down a different path than the one we planned on traveling down. Some of the world's greatest inventions have been discovered because something else failed to work as planned. Other failures will ultimately take us far beyond our dreams as they unfold to reveal new opportunities. Plus, the confidence and courage that you will feel as you adapt to new, stimulating scenarios will make each subsequent step on your new path less frightening or intimidating.

Like many women, you may discover an entirely new dream in the course of your pursuits. This could be something you can't even imagine right now, but if you don't start, you'll never know what it may be. At the very least, you will learn a lot about yourself, about life and about business – a success in itself! I know I've learned more in the past few years than I did in the previous twenty!

The relationships that I've built, all with positive, affirming people who have quickly become friends, make my journey exhilarating and rewarding. I've become more flexible and have even learned to embrace technology. I always joke with friends that I am so smart now, although I know that I'm not as knowledgeable as I'm going to be next year or the year after that! I love learning new ideas and having the courage to embrace new opportunities with enthusiasm.

You Can Always Go Back – Though You Never Will

Imagine inflating a balloon. The small piece of rubber expands, similar to how your mind expands when new ideas are introduced. Then, let the air out of the balloon. It is empty now, yet it no longer looks like it did before you inflated it.

Our minds are just like that balloon, capable of great expansion. Even if we dismiss that new idea, our mind will never be the same once a new idea has caused it to expand - just like that balloon. We need to continually challenge ourselves, our thoughts, and our minds, with new ideas and concepts, new opportunities, and new relationships. Without growth and inspiration, our minds stagnate. We have an obligation to ourselves to pursue exciting new courses and activities. We have an obligation to the universe to try new things, for when we conform, we contribute nothing new to our world. We remain ordinary, and that's a tragedy. Think of all the marvelous inventions of the past 20 years and imagine life without them. Aren't you glad someone took a leap and tried something new?

When you are about to change direction and try something new, know that the WORST thing that can happen will probably not be as bad as you imagined. Besides, you could probably retreat to your jumping off point (if necessary) without much suffering.

You may know someone who tried to make a new start, only to end up returning to their original job. Not only is there no harm done, but at least they won't have to live the rest of their lives filled with regret, wondering what might have happened if they had given their dreams a shot. Their "balloon" had been inflated and they may even begin working toward their next new venture.

Ask any successful entrepreneur, and they will probably tell you that their first idea failed or that they didn't find their true success until after several attempts were made. You may have to first learn new ways NOT to do something! These unique individuals took a leap of faith at some point in their lives and are now enjoying the rewards of their efforts. What's stopping you from joining them?

A PMA, or Positive Mental Attitude, will help to take you far. Remain optimistic and positive about any new venture, and you'll be surprised at the support you will attract!

Reasons Against Becoming an Entrepreneur

Why isn't everyone trying to build their own business? Are they afraid, undercapitalized, or just lazy? Here are some of the reasons people stay stuck merely *wishing* they could pursue their dream:

- They prefer to take a familiar path; it can be scary outside one's comfort zone!
- It's easier to work for someone else, free from responsibility.
- They are paralyzed by the fear of not knowing what to expect or what their new life could hold.
- They don't think they can financially afford to try.
- They suffer from a lack of discipline.
- Criticism from well-meaning friends and family.

This last point is critical. If you need everyone's approval before you begin a new venture, you may never move forward. Friends and family may not understand your motives or desires. You should not feel the need to explain it to them. They may also have an angle in wanting to keep you right where you are: If YOU become successful, where does that leave THEM? They may end up feeling inadequate, alone, or even jealous of your success.

You may have to share less of what's going on in your life with friends and family. I found that many of the people with whom I shared my dreams attempted to dilute or diminish them completely. You are done before you begin when the people you love and trust fail to give you the necessary support. You may need to speak in vague terms, simply sharing that your business is "coming along." You may also need to find some new friends! You will discover that some things that used to hold meaning for you will become less important while others take on new importance.

I found that as I moved forward in my life, in a new, different direction, my choices seemed to disturb almost everyone I knew! They couldn't understand what I was doing. Of course now that I'm successful in a new field, they all confirm that they "knew" I could do it! Actions speak louder than words, and the best way to tell someone what you intend to do is by doing it. So, what are you waiting for?

The Best Thing That Can Happen

Finally, we need to look at the BEST thing that can happen: *You can achieve your dreams!* Here are some of the side effects that pursuing your dreams may cause:

- Finding yourself - whether you felt lost in the first place or not!
- Feeling happier and more satisfied than you ever imagined you could be
- Unbelievable highs from experiencing new successes
- Learning that mistakes are merely lessons…stepping stones to your future

What are you waiting for? The worst thing that can happen is that your life will come and go and you will never know what you missed. Your journey as an entrepreneur will be positive, no matter what happens. You won't fail; you'll discover inner strength you didn't know you had as you experience new adventures. You'll expand your mind and contribute new ideas to the universe. You can do it…make the leap!